Culture and Resistance

Culture and Resistance
Conversations with Edward W. Said

David Barsamian
and
Edward W. Said

Haymarket Books
Chicago, Illinois

© 2019 David Barsamian and Edward W. Said

Originally published by South End Press in 2003.

This edition published in 2019 by
Haymarket Books
P.O. Box 180165
Chicago, IL 60618
773-583-7884
www.haymarketbooks.org
info@haymarketbooks.org

ISBN: 978-1-60846-582-8

Distributed to the trade in the US through Consortium Book Sales and Distribution (www.cbsd.com) and internationally through Ingram Publisher Services International (www.ingramcontent.com).

This book was published with the generous support of Lannan Foundation and Wallace Action Fund.

Special discounts are available for bulk purchases by organizations and institutions. Please call 773-583-7884 or email info@haymarketbooks.org for more information.

Cover design by Josh MacPhee.

Printed in the United States.

Library of Congress Cataloging-in-Publication data is available.

Table of Contents

Acknowledgments		vii
Foreword by David Barsamian		ix
Introduction by David Barsamian		xiv
1	A One-State Solution	1
2	Intifada 2000: The Palestinian Uprising	31
3	What They Want Is My Silence	71
4	Origins of Terrorism	103
5	A Palestinian Perspective on the Conflict with Israel	133
6	At the Rendevous of Victory	159
	Maps	197
	Selected Bibliography	211
	Index	215
	About the Authors	227
	Alternative Radio's Audio Archives	228

Acknowledgments

Excerpts of these interviews appeared originally in *The Progressive, Z Magazine, Third World Resurgence*, and *International Socialist Review*. All the interviews were broadcast on KGNU in Boulder, Colorado, one of the premier community radio stations in the United States. It has been my good fortune to be associated with it since it first went on the air in 1978. Two of the interviews were nationally broadcast on Alternative Radio and one on Making Contact. Except for chapters 1, 4 and 5, the interviews were all done in person. Anthony Arnove is an outstanding editor and comrade. Thanks to the Lannan Foundation in Santa Fe for its support. Thanks to Dr. Mahdi Abdul Hadi, chairman of the Palestinian Academic Society for the Study of International Affairs (PASSIA) in Jerusalem for the maps and Rebecca Kandel for the photos used here. My special gratitude to Edward W. Said for making himself available. I count my time with him among my most rewarding experiences.

Foreword

David Barsamian

Edward Said frequently came under attack for his solidarity with the oppressed, especially Palestinians. He told me it came with the territory. In their book *The Israel Lobby,* John Mearsheimer and Stephen Walt cite Jonathan Cole, former provost of Columbia University, saying, "One can be sure that any public statement in support of the Palestinian people by the preeminent literary critic Edward Said will illicit hundreds of e-mails, letters, and journalistic accounts that call on us to denounce Said and to either sanction or fire him."

Since *Culture and Resistance* was first published, as Said predicted, the situation for Palestinians has become appreciably worse. The landscape in some ways has never been bleaker.

Gaza has been invaded and bombed multiple times, with appalling casualties. Israeli colonies, described in the corporate media as settlements, have greatly expanded, swallowing up more land and siphoning off more water.

Including East Jerusalem, the number of Israelis colonizing Palestinian land now exceeds 600,000, a number that the Israeli government works relentlessly to increase.

The Trump administration has moved the U.S. Embassy in Israel from Tel Aviv to Jerusalem, a longstanding goal of the extreme right wing in Israel and among its ardent supporters in the United States.

The Palestinian leadership in Ramallah remains ineffectual, unimaginative, and sclerotic. Anniversaries come and go: twenty-five years since the Oslo Accords (that Said so presciently called the "Palestinian Versailles," forty years since the Camp David agreement, fifty years since the Six-Day War.

Multiple peace processes are all process and no peace, endless road maps that lead to dead ends. And in Washington there is a regime more tightly yoked to Israel than any other in U.S. history. In a way, it's salutary as there can be no "honest broker" illusions.

At the same time, Palestinians and the many people globally who stand in solidarity with them have cause for some measured optimism. The Boycott, Divestment, and Sanctions (BDS) movement has attracted more attention and adherents. The mood on campuses across the county has shifted dramatically.

Said would have been a strong supporter of the BDS movement as a counter to what he called, in his foreword to Eqbal Ahmad's *Confronting Empire,* our "endless surrenders and humiliations."

Foreword

xi

Said had no illusions about the difficult position Palestinians were in being the "victim of the victim," as he once told me.

In our first book together, *The Pen and the Sword*, also published by Haymarket Books, I asked Said about the great Italian radical Antonio Gramsci and his often quoted phrase, "pessimism of the intellect, optimism of the will." Said replied,

> They have to be linked causally. I say pessimism of the intellect first and then optimism of the will based on the pessimism of the intellect. In other words, you can't just say, things are bad, but never mind, I'm going to go forward. You have to say things are bad, and analyze them intellectually. And on the basis of that analysis you construct a movement forward based on optimism, the ability and the desire and the wish to change things.

Referring to the 1993 Oslo Accords, he continued:

> I find it's not the case here, where there's optimism right at the beginning of trying to turn, by magical process, what in effect is a disastrous agreement into a wonderful thing. They're saying it's parity, an opening, a foot in the door, it's going to change everything. That strikes me as irresponsible. That's not optimism of the will. That's magical thinking. Gramsci was very careful always to say that his work represented secular work and that these were parts of what he called the conquest of civil society. We haven't done the secular work yet. We have a long way to go. But I think it will happen. As Palestinians begin to rub their noses in the realities of this agreement and come up against the intransigence of the Israeli occupation, which

is going to continue, they're going to understand that the only way forward is continued resistance.

The struggle for justice for Palestine and Palestinians continues. In response to the many challenges of our present moment, Edward Said would say, be creative. Create new forms of resistance and interventions. Think outside the box. And don't forget the importance of culture in resistance.

He would often quote the poem "Under Siege" by the great Palestinian poet Mahmoud Darwish:

> *Here on the slopes of hills, facing the dusk and the cannon*
> *of time*
> *Close to the gardens of broken shadows,*
> *We do what prisoners do,*
> *And what the jobless do:*
> *We cultivate hope.*

Introduction

"I have been unable," Edward W. Said writes, "to live an uncommitted or suspended life: I have not hesitated to declare my affiliation with an extremely unpopular cause."[1]

The 1967 Arab-Israeli war stirred him to political activism. A year later, his first political essay, "The Arab Portrayed," appeared. When Israeli Prime Minister Golda Meir infamously declared in 1969, "It was not as though there was a Palestinian people.... They did not exist," Said decided to take on "the slightly preposterous challenge of disproving her, of beginning to articulate a history of loss and dispossession that had to be extricated, minute by minute, word by word, inch by inch," he writes.[2]

For many years, he has been the main spokesman for the Palestinian cause in the United States.

"Palestine," he says, "is a thankless cause ... [Y]ou get nothing back but opprobrium, abuse, and ostracism.... How many friends avoid the subject? How many colleagues want none of Palestine's controversy? How many *bien pensant* liberals have time for Bosnia and Chechnya and Somalia and Rwanda and South Africa and Nicaragua and Vietnam and human and civil rights everywhere on Earth, but not for Palestine and Palestinians?"[3]

He has paid a price for his high profile on the Palestinian issue. He was vilified as "the professor of terror." The Jewish Defense League called him a Nazi. His office at Columbia was set on fire, and both he and his family "received innumerable death threats," he writes.[4]

For more than a decade, Said was a member of the Palestine National Council (PNC), where he incurred the wrath of Arab nationalists because he advocated the "idea of coexistence between Israeli Jews and Palestinian Arabs" and because he recognized that "no military option exists." He writes, "I was also very critical of the use of slogan-clichés like 'armed struggle' and of the revolutionary adventurism that caused innocent deaths and did nothing to advance the Palestinian case politically."[5]

Since resigning from the PNC in 1991, Said has become one of the most public critics of Yasir Arafat and the so-called peace process. His was a rare voice of resistance amid all the euphoria when the Oslo Accords were signed on the South Lawn of the White House in September 1993. He understood instantly what Oslo meant and called it "a Palestinian Versailles."[6]

"There was Clinton like a Roman emperor bringing two vassal kings to his imperial court and making them shake hands," he told me.[7]

Parallel to his political activism is his enormous contribution to the humanities. With *Orientalism,* Said transformed the

Introduction xv

way we look at literary representations of Islam, Arabs, and the Middle East. He also explored the way knowledge is used to legitimize and defend power. *Culture and Imperialism,* which came out in 1993, and *Orientalism* form the bookends to his great cultural work.

Somehow, in his spare time, this Renaissance man has time to play piano and write about music and opera. He is inspired by and likes to quote from an Aimé Césaire poem:

> but the work of man is only just beginning
> and it remains to man to conquer all
> the violence entrenched in the recesses of his passion.

> And no race possesses the monopoly of beauty,
> of intelligence, of force, and there
> is a place for all at the rendezvous
> of victory.[8]

Poetry, incidentally, may have turned the trick for me the first time I interviewed him. We met in his office at Columbia and I was a bit nervous. My anxiety was not eased when he asked me at the outset if I had any good questions. It was when I mentioned a couplet by Mahmoud Darwish, the leading contemporary Palestinian poet, we began to hit it off. In the ensuing years, we did a series of interviews that resulted in *The Pen and the Sword,* a collection published by Common Courage Press in 1994.

It's hard to convey on the printed page the tremendous energy, intellectual excitement, and enthusiasm Said generates. He relishes the give and take of exchanges. Readers may xvi Culture and Resistance

be interested to know that all of his answers were spontaneous. We had not rehearsed or gone over any of the questions.

Since the early 1990s, Said has been battling leukemia. He is in and out of hospitals, about to begin treatments or recovering from them. Through it all, he manages to write and lecture. His opponents want him silent. But as he says in one of the interviews in this book, "Unless I die it's not going to happen."[9]

Notes

1   Edward W. Said, "Between Worlds," *London Review of Books* 20: 9 (May 7, 1998). See also Edward W. Said, *Out of Place: A Memoir* (New York: Knopf, 2000).

2   Edward W. Said, "The Arab Portrayed," in Ibrahim Abu-Lughod, ed., *The Arab-Israeli Confrontation of June 1967: An Arab Perspective* (Evanston: Northwestern University Press, 1970), pp. 1–9. See also Said, "Between Worlds," and Noam Chomsky, *Fateful Triangle: The United States, Israel, and the Palestinians*, updated ed. (Cambridge: South End Press, 1999), p. 51.

3   Edward W. Said, "Cherish the Man's Courage," in Eqbal Ahmad, *Eqbal Ahmad: Confronting Empire*, interviews with David Barsamian (Cambridge: South End Press, 2000), p. xxviii.

4   Said, "Between Worlds."

5   Said, "Between Worlds."

6   Edward W. Said, "A Palestinian Versailles," *The Progressive* 57: 12 (December 1993): 22–26.

7   Edward W. Said, Interview with David Barsamian, *The Progressive* 63: 4 (April 1999).

8   Aimé Césaire, "At the Rendezvous of Victory," trans. C.L.R. James, quoted in Edward W. Said, *Culture and Imperialism* (New York: Knopf, 1993), p. 280. Edward W. Said, "A Palestinian Versailles,"

22–26. David Barsamian, Interview with Edward W. Said, *The Progressive* 63: 4 (April 1999):34–38.

9 See p. 82.

A One-State Solution

KGNU, Boulder, Colorado, February 8, 1999

It is clear that Yasir Arafat is not well. He shakes and looks drawn. What reports do you get on his health?

His loyal supporters, one of whom I saw last week quite by chance—we were on the same plane—say that he's in perfect health. He just has this little shake, this little tremor. Others, including a physician who lives in Gaza and has seen him, are convinced that he has Parkinson's disease. But everyone I've spoken to in the last year who's seen Arafat, I haven't seen him, say that he's considerably slowed down and he's not as alert or as perky as he once was. So I suppose that's true. The fact is, however, that he still is in command of everything. He signs every little piece of paper involving employees' vacations, the movement of large funds, state documents. Everything has to go past his desk. He's still a micromanager. He shows no sign of delegating authority in any serious way. Most of his employees bad-mouth him, including his ministers. But they're powerless to do anything.

2   **Culture and Resistance**

I think it's important to note something that people may not be aware of, that he is the largest single employer in the Palestinian territories. In addition to an enormous bureaucracy, Arafat's security apparatus is numbered at 40,000.[1] This is a very unproductive segment of the economy. Plus the fact that there is, again thanks to his spending habits, no serious investment in infrastructure. So it's a stagnant situation which is, in my opinion, getting worse every day, largely due to his methods, which are essentially to retain control and to make sure that there are no opponents or changes in the structure, which is largely dictated to him, as it was in the case of Jordan, by the Israelis and the United States.

Your books were banned in Arafat's realm. Is that still the case?

It's difficult to know, actually. You can buy them. They're available surreptitiously, and they circulate, because in an age of e-mail, photocopying, and faxes, nothing can really be banned. But as recently as a year ago when I was there, I was recognized by a grocer who is also a bookseller. He told me, "I have your books, but I keep them under the counter, just in case some member of the Authority comes by." This was in Hebron. To make matters even more ironic and peculiar, a year after they were banned by order of the Minister of Information, Yasir Abed Rabbo, whose name was affixed to the edict, he wrote me a letter asking me if they could enter into an arrangement with me whereby they could publish my books on the West Bank.[2] You figure it out. I can't.

A One-State Solution

What about in Israel?

They're available.

And other Arab countries?

It depends. I haven't done a survey. They're mostly available in Egypt and Lebanon. I've heard reports that some of my books have been banned in Jordan and others in various countries of the Gulf. But that's the fate of everyone. We're talking about autocracies and despotisms, where there is no perceivable pattern. Somebody sees something that's offensive and they say, We can't have this. So they ban it. Or they'll ban an issue of a newspaper or magazine. So it's all very erratic. But I know from my Lebanese publisher that in some of the bigger Gulf countries, like Kuwait and Saudi Arabia, *Culture and Imperialism* is forbidden in Arabic. So it's a spotty picture. I think the same is true in Morocco and Tunisia. I don't know about Algeria. I don't think they're doing much importing of books just now.

Your critique of what is popularly called the "peace process" has been unrelenting since Oslo, September 1993. For years, the mainstream media, at least in the United States, pretty much have studiously ignored you. However, recently there's been a surge in terms of your visibility—Newsweek, the New York Times, National Public Radio, PBS, and other venues. What accounts for that?

I think that it's not just my critique, such as it has been, but that a lot of people now see the reality. Again, going back to the

4   **Culture and Resistance**

censorship model that we were just talking about, there's a form of censorship here in the United States, which is that you're marginalized. You can't appear in the mainstream media. But what also happens is that where you do appear—for example, in the Arab countries, my stuff appears on the Internet—it's picked up and people read it. When I got a request to write an article for the *New York Times Magazine* about my idea of a solution, a binational state, for Palestinians and Israelis, that was somebody who had read me on the Internet.[3] The editor called me up. Plus the fact that it was clear, he told me, that the peace process wasn't working, and neither, he said, was Zionism. For those reasons they turn their attention. But I don't think it's anything more than just a token kind of side look at, well, we want to be inclusive so we might as well include him. I think that's really what it is. Just looking at the media in general, particularly more recent things like the freezing of the peace process after the Wye agreement, the announcement of forthcoming Israeli elections, the death of King Hussein, etc., the old clichés, the old stereotypes, the old discourse, which is a system, is absolutely in place, untouched by reality or facts. It's quite striking. They seem to be unaware that there's anything going on. I remember appearing once on *The Charlie Rose Show* on PBS.[4] He kept repeating the prevailing wisdom at me and didn't let me finish my sentences. What I was saying was so outrageous that he couldn't allow it to be said in a certain way.

A One-State Solution

Why are you calling for a binational state now?

This is the first time in my life, since I left Palestine at the end of 1947, that I've been to the West Bank and Gaza and Israel on a regular basis. I went five times in the last year. The more I go, the more impressed I am with the fact that Israeli Jews and Palestinians are irrevocably intertwined demographically. That's the first thing that strikes you. The Israelis have a mania for building roads. A lot of them on the West Bank and Gaza go around Palestinian towns and villages. But nonetheless, the place is so small that you can't possibly completely avoid the other side. Second, Palestinians are employed by Israelis to build and expand West Bank and Gaza settlements. It's one of the greatest ironies of all. The Palestinians are workers in restaurants inside Israel in places like Tel Aviv and West Jerusalem and Haifa. And of course on the West Bank, where the settlers are, in towns especially like Hebron, but obviously Jerusalem and its environs, which include large Palestinian towns, like Beit Hanina, which were never part of Jerusalem but have become part of the municipal boundaries of the city, Palestinians and Israelis interact, through antipathy and hostility, but physically they're in the same place. Somehow being very impressed with what I can see and what I know to be a fact suggests to me that this is something that can't be changed by pulling people back to separate boundaries or separate states. The involvement of each in the other, largely, due to the aggressiveness with which the Israelis have entered the Palestinian territory, and from the very beginning

6　　　　　　**Culture and Resistance**

have invaded Palestinian space, suggests to me that some mode of arrangement has to be established that allows them to live together in some peaceable form. It's not going to be through separation.

Another factor which I think is very important is that there is a younger generation of Palestinians who are Israeli citizens, led by Knesset member Azmi Bishara. They have lived with Israeli Jews, as second-class citizens or in some instances as non-citizens when it comes to things like immigration and land ownership. They are acutely aware of the difficulty that they face as an oppressed minority and are beginning to struggle in terms of civil and citizens' rights. They are, interestingly, supported—implicitly, not actually—by secular Israelis who are quite worried about the increased power of the clerics and the whole question of defining the laws of the state by religious means in this debate about, Who is a Jew? and the power of the Orthodox over the Conservative and Reform movements. All of that has crystallized a fairly important, although again never mentioned by the media in this country, body of opinion that is secular and is beginning to talk about things like a constitution, since Israel doesn't have one, and the notion of citizenship, which defines people not by ethnic but by national criteria, which would then have to include Arabs. That's very impressive to me. I've talked to groups from both sides, independently and together. There the trajectory is unmistakable.

The fourth factor which brought this forth, the background of course being the failure of Oslo and the bank-

A One-State Solution

ruptcy of the vision of Netanyahu and Arafat and Clinton, is the demographic reality, which is that by the year 2010 there will be demographic parity between Palestinians and Israelis.[5] I'm not talking about all the Jews in the world or all the Palestinians in the world. I'm just talking about the people who are there. It's such a small territory. The South Africans in a country twenty times bigger couldn't for long maintain apartheid. It's unlikely that Israel, which is surrounded of course on all sides by Arab states, is going to be able to maintain what in effect is a system of apartheid for Palestinians when Palestinians are equal in number with them and if you add the other Palestinians and the other Arabs in the region, vastly outnumber them.

So I think taking all these factors into account, although it now seems like a totally long shot and completely utopian, not to say to many people a crazy idea, it is the one idea, a vision based on equality, that will allow people to live and not exterminate each other. Hopefully I was trying to stimulate discussion and reflection on the various modes by which such a state could exist or come about.

Your vision of inclusion and the one-state solution actually resonates with one of the old streams of Zionism.

As many Palestinians have, I've read the history of debates within the Zionist settlers' movement. I want to use the phrase in the most catholic way. There were people of a fairly important caliber, such as Martin Buber, Judah Magnes, who was the first president of Hebrew University, Hannah Arendt,

8   **Culture and Resistance**

and a few others who were not so well-known, these are the international luminaries, who realized that there was going to be a clash if the aggressive settlement policies and the unreflecting ignoring of the Arabs pressed ahead. David Ben-Gurion actually said that there's no case in history where a people simply gives up and allows another people to take their territory over.[6] So they knew that there would be a conflict, especially Magnes, who really was an idealist.

The more one reads about him and reflects on him, he was a man way ahead of his time, and a remarkable spirit also. He was an American, interestingly. He said, "Let's try to think in terms quite morally and profoundly about the Arabs. Let's think in terms of their presence, not their absence." I find that, interestingly, that spirit in a sense is to be found in the work of the new Israeli historians, some of them explicitly, some of them implicitly, who have gone back over the national narrative of Israel and reexamined according to historical and archival sources the myth of Israel's independence and so-called liberation, and discovered how much of it was based on the denial or the effacement or the willful avoidance of the Arabs.[7] All that Israel has been able to do for the last fifty years is not, of course, to get security for itself. There is no security of that sort. But it has been maintaining a kind of holding operation by which the Arabs are simply kept out. Over time that can't work because of demographics and the fact that people don't give up if they're beaten down. They in fact hold on even more resolutely and more stubbornly.

A One-State Solution

So that's a new climate of opinion. I think you could see it as coming out of Zionism. I don't want to appear negative or critical of it. A lot of it is an intra-Jewish debate, not something that's taking place between Palestinians and Israelis. It's taking place within, as it did in the case of Magnes and Arendt and Buber, the Zionist or Jewish camp. There were attempts to reach Palestinians. But the situation was overall so polarized, and the British were playing such a Machiavellian role, and the leadership of the Zionist community, people like Berl Katznelson, David Ben-Gurion, Chaim Weizmann, and others, were also such clever politicians that these individuals, who in the end *were* individuals, really didn't have much of a chance. It was a rather restricted debate. I don't think one should overemphasize it.

I think now people like myself, who luckily don't have to face the daily pressures of living in either Israel or Palestine, but have time to reflect at some distance, can play a role in terms of seeking out discussion and debate, with their opposite numbers in the other camp. That's beginning to happen, more or less systematically. There are frequent dialogues, frequent conferences between Palestinian and Israeli intellectuals, not with an eye towards, as there have been for so many years, settling the problem in a governmental way, as an adjunct to the peace process. There's a lot of that that's gone on and led nowhere. This is a new kind of discussion. It's based upon fairly patient scholarship, and fairly careful and scrupulous archival work. It's not carried out by people with political ambitions. It's mostly academics and people who are removed

10   **Culture and Resistance**

from the mainstream in politics on both sides but who have a certain standing within their communities as academics and intellectuals. It's quite a new phenomenon. I don't think it's been too focused on by the media, which is completely obsessed with the failing peace process.

In Israel proper, Palestinians constitute about 20 percent of the total population.[8] In late 1998, you had occasion to speak to some of them in your mother's birthplace, Nazareth, in a place with the unlikely name of Frank Sinatra Hall.

It was financed by Frank Sinatra, who was a great supporter of Israel. I think it was in the 1970s. He was prevailed upon to give money for a facility in Nazareth, which is a predominantly Arab town. It has some Jews living in it, particularly in Upper Nazareth. The idea was that this should be a kind of sports facility where young Arabs and young Jews could get together and play basketball. This apparently didn't get very far, although the hall was built. It was then taken over by the Histadrut, the Israeli labor federation. Over time it evolved into a rentable facility. You could rent the hall for the evening or for some occasion. I noticed that it not only has this large hall, but also a coffee shop and a bar, a pool hall, places where people can gather.

Azmi Bishara arranged this as my first public encounter with Palestinians who are Israeli citizens. Obviously, it's a highly factionalized population. Wherever there are Palestinians, there are dozens and dozens of currents and parties. So this one represented basically his group of people, young and old, who support him, plus others who were curious, who had never seen me before and wanted to. It was an interesting evening. I was asked to talk about the history of my political opinions and how I arrived at the position I now hold. Not many people know that much about my opinions, not even I.

So it was an interesting exercise. Then it was basically a free-for-all. They could ask any questions they wanted. I was very impressed. You could see easily the reflection on them of currents and discussions and, being somebody who's interested in language, you could hear the accents of other Arab politics—Baath and Nasserite and Arab nationalist and Marxist—through some of the questions and comments. But I also noticed that there was a kind of independent tone, a language, which reflected the fact that these people had had a different experience from all the other Arabs. They live as members of the Palestinian minority, within the Jewish state. So they're much more familiar with Israel than any other Arab group I've ever faced. They have daily encounters, in the university, in the workplace, and so on.

That made it a much more interesting discussion. One could talk directly about Israel. There was no tiptoeing around questions of religion. Since Bishara himself is a former Marxist who is a social democrat now, but quite radical, most of the people in the room, in fact all of the ones that I heard from, were basically secular people. There may have been Islamic people there. But as is the case with other talks that I give in the Arab world, they're always there, and sometimes you can identify them by the women with their head-

12   **Culture and Resistance**

gear and the men with beards in places like Egypt. But one of the interesting patterns that I've noticed is that although I'm always ready for them to say something to me, being as I am secular and quite aggressive about religious politics, they never say anything. They rarely ask questions, and they rarely publicly confront me. That was the same in Nazareth. There was no Islamic tendency at all. Most of it was questions of information, what I felt about the peace process. And of course everybody wants to know what's the alternative, which is a difficult question to answer. But the main idea was to engage.

It's opened the door now for another trip I'm going to make in March, when I'm going to be in Nazareth for three days at a conference of Arab students and also in Nazareth at the Israeli Anthropological Association, which has asked me to give a keynote speech at their annual meeting. So I find it extremely valuable to branch out from the, to me, often confining spaces of the Arab and particularly Palestinian world, which are in a state of siege, and you can feel that. Everywhere I go, I notice a qualitative difference when it comes to generations. There's no question at all in my mind of a new courage and skepticism; intellectual curiosity is to be found across the board in people who are at the most in their upper twenties, as well as those who are obviously younger. It's quite different from anything that I've experienced in people of my generation and the one that came right after it.

A One-State Solution

Might that be attributed to their not being shell-shocked by al-Nakba, the catastrophe of 1948?

That has something to do with it. It also has to do with what I mentioned earlier. There is no underestimating it, and this has been a tremendous revelation to me, that people now read stuff that they couldn't have read as recently as five years ago, through the Internet, e-mail, and the ready availability of rapidly moving, you might say, *samizdat* that bypasses the official media, through all kinds of alternative sources, radio, television. Don't forget, this is a highly saturated part of the world when it comes to media. Most people get diverse information through satellite dishes. They get TV from Arab countries. They all get CNN. So they can compare. There's a tremendous variety. There's a much greater desire to explore, debate, and discuss alternatives, especially among young people. So I think from that point of view it's a much more hopeful situation than any one I've faced since 1967, in terms of exchange of opinions and the potential for political change in the future.

En route to your destination in Nazareth, you had occasion to pick up a young West Bank Palestinian hitchhiker. You had a rather revealing exchange.

That was a young man who comes from a village not far from Jericho. I was traveling from Ramallah to Nazareth via Afula, which is an Israeli town inside the Green Line. We picked him up just outside Nablus. He turned out to be a croupier in training at the new Palestinian casino, which is

14   **Culture and Resistance**

one of these incredible anomalies that the peace process has brought forth. He was in training and therefore commutes by hitchhiking. He explained to us that in a few weeks, when his training was over, he was going to have to live there because they were building housing for the staff of this casino. The casino is largely an Austrian operation, although Arafat's Authority has a 30 percent share in it.[9] Its main customers are Israelis, since gambling is not allowed in Israel. They go over there and spend a lot of money on blackjack and roulette and baccarat. The foreign workers live in an Israeli settlement, which is not far away, as does the director.

So you have the extraordinary conjuncture of an obviously totally unproductive casino, foreign-owned and directed, Palestinian-supported. Of course, the money goes back into the Authority. It isn't spent on the Palestinian people. And a small group of Palestinians from neighboring villages—I thought it was interesting that he was a member of the Christian minority, this croupier—work there and cater to rich Israelis and foreigners, and I suppose rich Palestinians, too, who come there and spend their money. In time, I was led to understand, they would have bowling alleys and a swimming pool. I must say that Jericho is one of the last places you'd think of to have a casino. It's in the lowest, from the point of view of sea level, spot on earth, and the heat in summer must be 140 degrees in the shade. It's not the kind of place you naturally gravitate to. But it strikes me as the kind of fruit of the current incoherence of what is being offered to

A One-State Solution 15

both Israelis and Palestinians as the future. It's not a very hopeful sign.

The casino has come under scrutiny by no less than Suha Arafat, Yasir Arafat's wife. She called it a "disgrace" in a front-page New York Times *article. "I hate it," she said. "It's the most shameful act that the economic counselors of the Palestinian Authority did. Right across from a refugee camp, no less. We have no hospitals, no sewage, sick children, a whole sick society. But, oh, we have gambling. Great."[10]*

She's a mixed bag. She drives around Gaza in her blue BMW. She spends a lot of time in Paris. She has an apartment on the Ile St. Louis and has Parisian hairdressers and couturiers. Her family is in business. I don't quite understand what the new persona of Suha Arafat is except to deflect attention a little bit from the egregiousness of the whole situation. Certainly what she says is true, but it isn't to say that she and various members of Arafat's retinue don't continue to play a role in this kind of corruption.

After you visited Israel, you went to Egypt, where you encountered some parochialism. Did that take you by surprise?

No, because I've confronted it before. That is to say, what you notice amongst Palestinians, whether inside Israel or on the West Bank and Gaza, is a sense of isolation. There's no question that they live under the shadow of Israeli power. What is missing is easy and natural contact with the rest of the Arab world. As a Palestinian, you can't get to any place in the Arab world from Israel or the West Bank and Gaza without

16   **Culture and Resistance**

going through a fairly complicated procedure, which causes you to think three or four times before you do it: crossing the border, you need permits, you go through endless customs. I must say, for Palestinians traveling throughout the Arab world—and this is also true of me, and I have an American passport, but the fact that it says on it that I was born in Jerusalem means that I'm always put to one side—you're automatically suspected. So traveling and being in contact with Arabs in the Arab world for Palestinians is very difficult.

More important even than that is that very few Arabs who are not Palestinians come into the Palestinian territories, and hardly any at all, practically none, go to Israel. One of the themes—and this is kind of a complicated thing to explain, amongst the nationalist and radical intellectuals of most Arab countries, which would include the Gulf people, it certainly includes Egypt, Syria, Lebanon, Jordan—has been the opposition to what they call "normalization," *tatbee* in Arabic, meaning the normalization of life between Israel and, in the case of Jordan and Egypt, Arab states who have made formal peace with Israel. The peace with Egypt is described, as it is with Jordan, as a cold peace. In other words, ordinary Jordanians or Egyptians, don't go to Israel, have nothing to do with Israelis. Israeli tourists go to Jordan and Egypt and visit the historic sites in buses for short periods of time. But beyond that, there's very little in the way of the kind of intercourse, say, exchanges between universities, learned societies, businesses, and so on, that occur between European countries or neighboring countries otherwise at peace in any other

A One-State Solution

part of the world. One of the reasons for this has been the general refusal, as an act of solidarity with Palestinians, of these intellectuals to have anything to do with Israel.

The problem this poses for Palestinians, trying to build institutions, is they are being cut off from the kind of help they can get from Arabs. For example, physicians and other medical professionals from Egypt, Syria, Lebanon, or Jordan could come and assist Palestinians in setting up clinics and hospitals. They could be involved in a whole range of activities from administration to the production of pharmaceuticals. But it doesn't happen because of this stance against normalization. Similarly, university students who read important scholars, journalists, writers, and poets from various Arab countries don't get the opportunity to meet them.

When I now encounter Arabs and go to these Arab countries, I say to them, especially to the Egyptians, you can go to Palestine. You can go through Israel, because Israel and Egypt are at peace. You can take advantage of that to go to Palestinians and go to their institutions and help them, appearing, speaking, being there for some time, training them. No, they say, we can't possibly allow our passports to be stamped. We won't go to the Israeli embassy and get visas. We won't submit to the humiliation of being examined by Israeli policemen at the border or the barrier.

I find this argument vaguely plausible on one level but really quite cowardly on the other. It would seem to me that if they took their pride out of it, if they did go through an Israeli checkpoint or barricade or border, they would be doing what

18 **Culture and Resistance**

other Palestinians do every day and see what it's like. Second, as I keep telling them, by doing that it's not recognizing Israel or giving Israel any credit. On the contrary, it's going through that in order to demonstrate and be with Palestinians and help them. For example, as Palestinians face the Israeli bulldozers as they expropriate land and destroy houses for settlements, it would be great if there were a large number of Egyptians and Jordanians and others who could be there with Palestinians confronting this daily, minute-by-minute threat. And the same in the universities. Well-known writers, intellectuals, historians, philosophers, film stars could go, but they say, We don't want to have to request visas from the Israeli consulate in Cairo. I said, You don't even have to do that. You can ask the Palestinian Authority, which has an ambassador in Cairo, to give you an invitation to go to Gaza, and then you can go to the West Bank.

So there are ways of getting around it. It's not so much only parochialism as also a kind of laziness, a kind of sitting back and expecting somebody else to do it. I think that's our greatest enemy, the absence of initiative. We're always expecting that the Israelis are out there, the Americans, concocting conspiracies, the Ford Foundation. Many people want to work with these groups but are afraid to do it publicly. They do it surreptitiously. And in public they express opposition and say, We are going to remain untouched by this. We are not going to normalize. We refuse to have anything to do with imperialism. We refuse to sit down and plan something that could actually help Palestinians and actually

A One-State Solution 19

deal with Israel, not as a fictional entity but as a real power that is in many ways negatively affecting Arab life.

For me, the great symbol of this is the fact that in no university that I know of in the Arab world—none of these universities are free in any case, they're all highly politicized and there are all kinds of pressures on professors and students, which is quite obvious—but in no important Arab university is there, for example, a department of Israeli studies, nor do people study Hebrew. And this is true even of Palestinian universities, where again, you can understand it as a kind of defense against this great power which has intervened in all of our lives, that we don't want to have anything to do with it. But for me the only salvation is in fact to encounter it head-on, learn the language, as so many Israeli political scientists and sociologists and Orientalists and intelligence people spend time studying Arab society. Why shouldn't we study them? It's a way of getting to know your neighbor, your enemy, if that's what it is, and it's a way of breaking out of the prison which suits the Israelis perfectly to have Arabs in, whether Palestinians or others.

I think it extends, alas, this passivity, this provincialism, extends not just to Israel on the part of the Arab world, but to countries other than America. There's this mania, this obsession in the Arab world about *the* West, *the* United States, Harvard, Samuel Huntington, Clinton, Monica Lewinsky, and all the rest of it. All of it done through the most simple-minded, the most vulgar of media presentations, but very little attention paid to India, Japan, China, to the great civilizations of

20   **Culture and Resistance**

the rest of the world. You go to a university like that of Amman. I can guarantee you won't find anybody studying Africa or Latin America or Japan. And it's a sign of our, as a society, as a people, in the moment in history in which we find ourselves, of our deliquescence, our weakness, our state of intellectual quiescence, that we are so uncurious about these other parts of the world.

One of the things that I try to do, in a very uncompromising and quite open way, is to say, We have to break that attitude. We have to break out of our self-constructed mind-forged manacles and look at the rest of the world and deal with it as equals. There's too much defensiveness, too much sense of aggrieved, unfulfilled whatever. This in part accounts for the absence of democracy. It's not just the despotism of the rulers, not just the plots of imperialism, it's not just the corrupt regimes, not just the secret police. It's our intellectuals' lack of citizenship, in the end, and that's a very important thing to emphasize and keep insisting on. For myself, since there is little I can do at this distance, whether in person or through my writing, is to keep making that point. The only way to change a situation is oneself doing it, reading, asking, encountering, breaking out of the prison.

One of the things you stress is the need for Israelis to acknowledge what they did to your people, the Palestinians. Why is that so important?

Because so much of our history has been occluded. We are invisible people. The strength and power of the Israeli narrative is such that it depends almost entirely on a kind of

A One-State Solution

21

heroic vision of pioneers who come to a desert and in the end deal not with native people in the sense that these are people who have a settled existence and lived in towns and cities and have their own society, but rather with nomads who could be driven away. The construction of the figure of the nomad was a very complex procedure, but it was certainly used by the Zionists to deal with us as a people. From many Israelis I've spoken to, particularly of my generation, you realize that part of the establishment of the state—the education and formation of Israeli citizens in the 1950s and the 1960s—was precisely to construct this shutting out of the Palestinians. It's a very difficult thought to accept, that you are there not because you're a great, heroic figure escaping the Holocaust, but you are there largely at the expense of another person who you've displaced or killed or driven away.

It seems to me therefore absolutely crucial to achieve some kind of real normalization, where Israelis can become part of the Middle East and not an isolated sanctuary connected to the West exclusively and denying and contemptuous and ignorant of the Palestinians. One sign is that wherever you go in Israel, the road signs are written in English and Hebrew. There's no Arabic. So if you're an Arab and you can't read Hebrew or English, you're lost. That's design. That's a way to shut out 20 percent of the population. So it's very important for Israelis to be forced intellectually and morally to confront the realities of their own history.

This is a part to be played by the new historians, but it's also important that Palestinians do it directly to Israelis and say, This is the reality. I think it's one of the consequences of 1948, at this late date, five decades after it, that we can begin to talk about Palestinian and Israeli history together. Separate histories that can be seen as intertwined and counterpointed with each other. Without that, the Other is always going to be dehumanized, demonized, invisible. We must find a way. That's where the role of the mind, the role of the intellectual, the moral consciousness is crucial. There has to be a way properly to deal with the Other and render that Other a place, as opposed to no place. So it's very far from utopian. A utopia means no place. So this is a placing of the Other in a concrete history and space.

That's why I think the study of maps and geography and the construction of space is really crucial to all this, not only history, which one does anyway—one can construct narratives of a fairly imaginative kind—but looking at the actual spots. Moshe Dayan made a famous remark in the middle 1970s. He said, "There is not one place built in this country that did not have a former Arab population."[11] He was able to see it, and he said it. And he said, We took them by force. Don't forget that. But subsequent generations, partly through the effects of the closeness of the United States and the diaspora American Jewish community, have eroded the possibility of that sensibility. It's important for those of us who have freed ourselves from the constraints of dogma and orthodoxy and authority to take those steps and to show those places as they really are. And it's important for Arabs to understand, too, that these are not epiphenomena, like Cru-

A One-State Solution

saders or imperialists who can be sent back somewhere. It's very important for us also to insist, as I often do, that the Israelis are Israelis. They are citizens of a society called Israel. They're not "Jews," quite simply, who can be thought of once again as wanderers, who can go back to Europe. That vocabulary of transitory and provisional existence is one that one has to completely refuse.

Daniel Barenboim is a world-famous pianist and conductor who was born in Argentina, grew up as an Israeli. You've had some interesting musical interactions with him.

We met seven or eight years ago and quite surprisingly we've become close friends. He travels a great deal, as do I. Sometimes our paths have crossed. We've tried to do things. We've had public discussions, not political ones so much, because he's not a politician any more than I am, but we talk about things like music and culture and history. He's very interested as an Israeli or Jewish musician in the work of people like Wagner, who represents you might say, the total negation of Jews but was a great musician. So he's interested in that paradox whereby culture and music work in parallel and create contradictions at the same time. We're doing a book together based on that theme.[12] But he's also very dissatisfied, as am I, with the prevailing orthodoxy in his own community. He hasn't lived in Israel recently, and last year refused to do anything with the Israel Philharmonic for the fiftieth anniversary of Israel. He is very much opposed to the occupation of the West Bank. He speaks openly about a Palestinian state.

24 Culture and Resistance

He's a man of courage, an unorthodox personality. Music connects us, but also the facts of biography. He arrived in Palestine, or Tel Aviv, which is where his family lived, roughly about the time that my family was evicted.

We have a very warm and cordial relationship. I arranged recently for him, in fact last week, the first time ever, to play a recital at Bir Zeit, the leading West Bank university. It was a great gesture on his part. It took a long time to work out. There were all sorts of problems, not on his side. Bir Zeit was shut down by the Israelis for four years during the Intifada. The president had been deported for twenty years, between 1974 and 1994. Only a couple of months ago, a student was killed by Israeli troops near the campus. There's this long history of animosity and hostility between Bir Zeit and the Israelis.

So it was difficult to accept at first the idea of an Israeli coming to play there. But it worked over time, and it was a fantastic success. It was one of the great events of my life, and if I can speak for him, of his life, that he was able to do this and transcend in an act that was purely cultural but also a human act of solidarity and friendship, offering his services, which God knows in any concert hall in the world would be in tremendous demand and are very costly. He's at the very top of the musical profession as a great pianist and a great conductor. He came simply as an individual to play. He brought his own piano with him, since there are no pianos that are any good there, to play a recital for an essentially Palestinian audience, ironically, in the hall in the university called Kamal Nasser Hall, named after a cousin of the president,

A One-State Solution

who had been assassinated in Beirut in 1973. He was a very good friend of mine, and I was there when it happened. The assassination team was led by Ehud Barak, who is today a leader of the Labor Party and was an intelligence commando officer at the time.[13]

All of that gave the evening a very high emotional and I would say cultural resonance that was lost on absolutely no one there. Zubin Mehta came, a great friend of Daniel's. He's the conductor of the Israel Philharmonic. He's an Indian. He's avidly pro-Israeli. He'd never been to the West Bank. But he came. Tears were streaming down his face. It was an event of considerable importance, precisely because it wasn't political in the overt sense. Nobody was trying to make a killing, score a point. It was just a humane gesture, an act of solidarity based on the friendship between myself and Barenboim and a gradually expanding group of Palestinian friends who admire and like him and with whom he likes to be. He's taken the position, I think quite correctly, that if Israel is going to continue to exist it has to exist in relations of friendship and equality with Arabs and Muslims. He's desperately anxious to learn Arabic. He's a very unusual, remarkable, advanced case of a prophetic genius. There aren't too many of them around. I hope we can sustain this kind of activity over time.

Perhaps I should also mention that he and Yo-Yo Ma are doing something in Weimar this summer. Weimar is the cultural capital of Europe for 1999. We have this idea where we would bring gifted, mostly Arab, but some Israeli musicians between the ages of eighteen and twenty-five to Weimar for

26   Culture and Resistance

about ten days. Weimar, interestingly, is about an hour away from Buchenwald. So there's that history. Plus, of course, it's the city of Goëthe and Schiller and Liszt, the summit of German culture. And Weimar has something to do, because of Buchenwald, with the founding of Israel and the problem of the Palestinians and the existence of our diaspora and dispersion. So the idea is to have master classes with Daniel and Yo-Yo and musicians from the Berlin State Opera, which Daniel is the conductor of, and in the evening have discussions led by me on the relationships between culture, politics, history, and especially music. We've gotten some wonderful young musicians who have applied, sent in tapes, auditioned, and been accepted. It promises to be quite a fantastic experience for all of us.

The good thing about it, for me, at any rate, being the peculiar person that I am, is that there is no program. Nobody is going to sign a declaration at the end. It's just a kind of peculiar mix which has a kind of cultural center to it, and all sorts of unforeseen and possible consequences that may be political, but since none of us is a politician, we're not really that interested in that aspect of it. What we are interested in is the power of music and discussion and culture to create a sense of equality and fellowship otherwise unavailable to us in the anguish and tension of the polarized life of the Middle East.

A One-State Solution

It's been about eight years now since during a routine check on your cholesterol you discovered that you had leukemia. People want to know about your health. How are you feeling?

Thank you for asking. I've had bad periods of time. For the first three years I didn't need any treatment. Suddenly, in early spring of 1994, I began treatment, first chemotherapy and later radiation. All of which led to various kinds of infections and debilitating consequences which during 1997 and 1998 were very, very difficult for me. I was sick most of the time. I lost a lot of weight. I have a fantastic Indian doctor who is taking care of me. During the course of all of this, I discovered to my dismay that I have a very rare form of leukemia called refractory leukemia which resists all the known forms of chemotherapy. Last summer I did a twelve-week experimental treatment, called a monoclonal antibody, which was incredibly difficult to go through. I was sick the whole time, for twelve weeks. I did it three or four times a week. Happily, I have what is now called a temporary remission. It's not a cure. The disease comes back, but at least it's been able to give me six months so far without major treatment and general good health. I'm feeling good about it.

28   **Culture and Resistance**

Notes

1   Barton Gellman, "Netanyahu, Arafat Sign Accord," *Washington Post,* October 24, 1998, p. A1.

2   United Press International, "Palestinian Lawmaker Condemns Book Ban," August 23, 1996.

3   Edward W. Said, "The One-State Solution," *New York Times Magazine,* January 10, 1999, p. 6: 36–39.

4   Interview with Edward W. Said, *The Charlie Rose Show,* WNET-TV, June 6, 1996.

5   See Meron Benvenisti, "The Return of the Refugees Won't Tip the Scales," *Ha'aretz,* July 8, 1999.

6   See Simha Slapan, *Zionism and the Palestinians* (London: Croom and Helm, 1979), p. 143.

7   See, among other works, Benny Morris, *The Birth of the Palestinian Refugee Problem, 1947–1949* (Cambridge: Cambridge University Press, 1989); Avi Shlaim, *Collusion Across the Jordan: King Abdullah, the Zionist Movement, and the Partition of Palestine* (New York: Columbia University Press, 1988); and Ilan Pappe, *The Making of the Arab-Israeli Conflict, 1947–1951* (London: I.B. Taurus, 1992).

8   See Martin Sieff, "The Israeli Arabs—A Ticking Time Bomb," United Press International, October 2, 2000.

9   Deborah Sontag, "Arafat's Gamble: A Casino for an Israeli Clientele," *New York Times,* September 15, 1998, p. A4; Agence France-Presse, "Palestinian Authority Admits Squirreling Millions Away in Secret Slush Fund," July 5, 2000.

10   Deborah Sontag, "Suha Arafat: A Militant in a Blue BMW," *New York Times,* February 4, 1999, p. A1.

11   Edward W. Said, *The Question of Palestine,* 2nd ed. (New York: Vintage Books, 1992), p. 14.

12   Daniel Barenboim and Edward W. Said, *Parallels and Paradoxes: Explorations in Music and Society,* (New York: Pantheon Books, 2002)

13 John Kifner, "Israel's Silence Reinforces Belief Its Commandos Killed P.L.O. Aide," *New York Times,* April 18, 1988, p. A1.

Intifada 2000:
The Palestinian Uprising

New York, New York, November 9, 2000

In your writings and lectures on the Israeli-Palestinian conflict, you constantly refer to the centrality of 1948. What do people need to know about 1948?

I don't think you can understand what's happening today and the situation of the Palestinians unless you understand what happened in 1948. A society made up principally of Arabs in Palestine was uprooted and destroyed. An Arab population of 800,000 people was driven out by design. The Zionist archives are quite clear about this, and several Israeli historians have written about it.[1] Of course the Arabs have said it all along. By the end of the conflict in 1948, Palestinians were a minority in their own country. Two-thirds of them had become refugees, whose descendants today number about seven and a half million people scattered throughout the Arab world, Europe, Australia, and North America.[2] The balance of the people became subjects to Israeli military occupation in 1967,

32   **Culture and Resistance**

when the West Bank and Gaza, along with East Jerusalem, were taken over and occupied.

Nineteen forty-eight for Palestinians is the date on which their search for self-determination begins. It doesn't begin in 1967. That simply completed the Israeli conquest. During 1948, not only was all of the land of the Palestinians, roughly 94 percent, taken over militarily by the state of Israel as land for the Jewish people, which meant that the Arabs who remained, and who are now roughly 20 percent of the population of Israel, are not entitled to hold land. Most of the land in Israel is controlled by the state for the Jewish people. Second, 400-plus Arab villages were destroyed, which were then replanted, so to speak, by Israeli settlers who built the kibbutzim. Every kibbutz in Israel is on Arab property. So the festering wound of 1948 has remained, while at the same time Israel since 1948 has said, We bear no responsibility for what happened to the Palestinians. They left because their leaders told them to. All sorts of propaganda was used. Until now, there's been a general consensus that they were not driven out by the Israelis. Second, there's been no attempt by the Israelis ever, even during the last meetings at Camp David in July, to consider the right of return, the central demand of every Palestinian, that he or she be allowed to return to the place from which he or she was driven out in 1948.[3] That is the core of the whole thing.

Intifada 2000: The Palestinian Uprising

Talk about the framework of the public discourse. Start with the "peace process."

The peace process began in 1993, when a secret agreement was made between the PLO and the Israeli government to undertake to give the Palestinians and the Palestine Liberation Organization under Yasir Arafat some territory and authority in the West Bank and Gaza. However, given the tremendous disparity in power between the Israelis and the Palestinians, in effect the peace process has simply been a repackaging of the Israeli occupation. Even as we speak today, in November 2000, Israel still controls 60 percent of the West Bank and 40 percent of Gaza. It has annexed Jerusalem and has filled the territories with settlers. Including the ones in Jerusalem there are about 400,000 Israelis who are there illegally.[4] These are settlements and a military occupation that is the longest in the twentieth and twenty-first century, the longest formerly being the Japanese occupation of Korea from 1910 to 1945. So this is thirty-three years old, pushing the record.

Essentially, the peace process has simply involved the Palestinian leadership in accepting Israeli terms. A small redeployment of Israeli troops. The settlements continue. Jerusalem is still under Israeli sovereignty and settlement. The borders and the water are controlled by Israel. The exits and entrances are controlled by Israel. Security is controlled by Israel. What the Americans and Israelis were doing was getting Palestinian consent to this repackaging of the occupation. It's been presented to the public as moving towards peace,

34　　　　　　　　**Culture and Resistance**

whereas it's been a gigantic fraud. Only that could possibly explain the extent and depth of the Palestinian rebellion that has taken place since September 29, 2000.

What about the term "defense"?

Of course, the Israeli army is called the Israeli Defense Forces. The line has been that the Israeli army is a defensive one. Whereas in fact, very misleadingly, the media have presented them as if they are defending Israel from Palestinians, who are basically throwing stones. This has an almost Orwellian quality to it. The Palestinians have no arms to speak of, except for some small arms among the police. It's been a population of stone-throwing youths against Israeli missiles, jets, helicopter gunships, tanks, and rockets. The most important thing is that all the fighting has taken place on Palestinian territory. So to use the word "defense" here is a grotesque misnomer. This is an occupation force inside Palestinian territory. The Palestinians are resisting military occupation and the Israelis are prolonging the occupation, and making, as all colonial troops have done, whether in Algeria, Vietnam, or India, the civilian population pay the price of resistance.

How about "terrorism"?

It's a very ugly conflict and has been since the twenties, when the Zionists in effect introduced terrorism into Palestine. It was one of the standard techniques of the early groups of Zionist extremists, in the 1920s, who put bombs in Arab marketplaces to terrorize the population. This led to a cre-

Intifada 2000: The Palestinian Uprising　　35

scendo during the thirties and forties, when terrorism was used by the Zionists against the British to hasten their retreat from Palestine, which they of course did retreat from in 1948.

Since that time, there has been a great deal of back and forth. In all cases, it has to be remembered that despite the horrendous loss of life, and there is simply no way of excusing or making up for the innocents who have lost lives, there has been a vast preponderance of Palestinian losses. If you look at the example of the figures of the last six weeks, there have been 180 Palestinians killed and fourteen Israelis.[5] That gives you a sense of the distinction. Eight were soldiers. The Palestinians were all civilians. Terrorism in this context has been for the Palestinians the weapon of the weak and the oppressed. It has been very limited and sporadic, but amplified and blown up to grotesque proportions by the Israelis, who always try to portray themselves as the victims, whereas in fact in this conflict they are not the victims. They are the oppressors, the people who have aggressed against the Palestinians.

What about the frequent references to the United States as an even-handed, honest broker?

Israel is the only state in the world that has received U.S. military and economic aid that now roughly totals about $135 billion in today's dollars.[6] Every U.S. political figure of note, whether it's a campaigner in a small district in northern New York State or a presidential contender, has had to declare himself or herself an unconditional supporter of Israel. Declarations from the Congress, from either the Senate or the

36 Culture and Resistance

House of Representatives, automatically bring forth huge majorities in support of Israeli policy because of the power of the Israeli lobby and the fact that there is a very active and politically savvy and sensitively placed community of supporters of Israel. U.S. policy has really focused on the defense and support of Israel in all of its ventures. The United States has vetoed scores of UN Security Council resolutions to prevent censure of Israel in cases which are flagrant violations of international law, ranging from torture to using helicopters and missiles against civilians to settlements and illegal annexations.[7]

So to say that the United States is an even-handed broker is a preposterous mischaracterization. The United States is very much in Israel's camp. All the information we have on the negotiations during the last seven years of the peace process has shown that the United States has presented the Israeli point of view in the discussions and remains a partisan of Israel. It should also be mentioned, by the way, that most of the officials involved in the peace process, beginning with Dennis Ross, Martin Indyk, and Aaron David Miller are themselves former employees or long time partisans of the Israeli lobby.

The Economist, *the conservative British weekly, observed that "the new Palestinian Intifada is rapidly assuming the form of a serious anti-colonial revolt."* [8] *This might be the first use of that phrase in a mainstream magazine.*

I think there was an anti-colonial revolt before during the first Intifada, which took place in 1987 and was stopped by

Intifada 2000: The Palestinian Uprising

Arafat in 1993. This is certainly that. The occupation of the West Bank and Gaza with settlers and settlements and roads and the constant expropriation of Palestinian lands, the destruction of crops and olive trees to make way for roads, the redesigning of the geography of the West Bank to permit greater Israeli control, all these policies have, were it not for the amnesiac U.S. media, followed the line of all classical colonialism. That is to say, to make sure that an oppressed and subordinate people are captive in their subordination for the profit and in some cases the leisure of the occupiers.

So what has happened in the last six or seven weeks has been an attempt to overthrow this, including the peace process, which is, as I said, a form of repackaging of the occupation, streamlining it so that the Israelis can control without using so many troops, frequently using Palestinians to police the people on behalf of the Israelis. That's been part of the peace process. Ironically, a lot of the question of Israeli security has been handed over to Palestinian policemen, who have to subdue precisely the people who are now the anti-colonial demonstrators. This conflagration, this enormous loss of life, can only be the result of an occupation policy that has simply destroyed the lives of people, where their only alternative has been to take to the streets and courageously, some would say, in a foolhardy way, throw stones at tanks. Unafraid.

We recall in Tiananmen Square a few years ago the outcry, the world chorus of approval and support and admiration for the young Chinese who opposed the military tanks in Tiananmen Square. This has not happened here. The media

38   **Culture and Resistance**

are so preponderantly pro-Israeli that ordinary people are not able to voice their support for what in effect is a brave attempt to overthrow a colonial style military occupation.

You've pointed out that there are no maps in this most geographical of conflicts. Why are maps important?

First of all, Palestine itself, the whole area, is tiny. This conflict has been going on for fifty years. Given the notoriously small attention span of the average TV viewer or reader of newspapers, there's very little awareness of the history or the geographical topography that's been involved. Most people say, The Arabs and the Jews are back at it again, giving the notion that there are two equal sides and that one side, the Israeli side, is beset and victimized. The Arabs are the ones who are assaulting and threatening. And of course the memories of the Holocaust and all the horrors of anti-Semitism hover in the background. Whereas in fact what has happened is that for all Palestinians, 1948 and the founding of the state of Israel, meant that essentially 78 percent of historic Palestine that was Arab has become Israeli.[9] That's been conceded. The West Bank and Gaza together constitute 22 percent of historical Palestine, and this is what the current fight is over. The Palestinians are not fighting over the 78 percent that they've already lost. They're fighting over the 22 percent that remains. Of this 22 percent, the Israelis are still in control of 60 percent of the West Bank and 40 percent of Gaza. So if there was ever to be a Palestinian state, there would be no contiguous territory. It would all be chopped into little pieces,

Intifada 2000: The Palestinian Uprising

controlled by the roads which the Israelis have built and which are now encircling each of the Palestinian areas, which is why Palestinians today are besieged within their little territory.

The Israelis have created facts on the ground that make it impossible for Palestinians to move from one area to another, from north to south from east to west. "Greater Jerusalem," which is roughly 4 percent of the whole territory, has been annexed by Israel and the Israelis plan not to give it back at all.[10] The idea is that this area will be totally controlled by Israel except for municipal services and issues like health, all those problematic citizen problems that they want to give over to the Palestinian Authority. Security and borders are under Israeli control. Even today Yasir Arafat can't go in and out of Gaza without Israeli permission, and they can shut the airport, and even destroy it completely, as they have, and shut down the territory so that people can't move. In effect, they are being choked to death. This is the result of the peace process. This is not the result of war. This is part of the disaster of the agreement between the Israelis and the Palestinian leadership under the aegis of the United States, which is why it's blown up.

Where is your information coming from?

The *Report on Israeli Settlement in the Occupied Territories,* which is a bimonthly published in Washington.[11] The editor is Geoffrey Aronson. It's a publication of the Foundation for Middle East Peace. It's the single most authoritative source drawn from Israeli and Palestinian and international agencies

40 **Culture and Resistance**

on the rate of settlement building, the holding of settlements, the initiation of new settlements, the destruction of property, and the increase in the settler population.

Noam Chomsky, Alexander Cockburn, Robert Fisk, and other critics of Israeli settlement policy have used the term "bantustan" in describing it.[12]

There's a kind of repeatable quality to this. It comes from the history of nineteenth-century colonialism. The French did this in Algeria. They would find areas where docile natives could be put in their villages with native chiefs. In West Africa the British did it under what was called "indirect rule," where they could find certain indigenous people to rule the unruly natives—and you as the occupying power held the real authority. In South Africa, the idea was to put the blacks on reservations or homelands where they could have some of the attributes of sovereignty but none of the real ones. They couldn't control the land. The water was not under their control. The entrances and exits were controlled by the whites. This is exactly the pattern here. These little Palestinian areas, which are small and divided, are centers of Palestinian population, but they are the equivalent of homelands where somebody like Arafat could have the impression, or give himself the impression, that he's the leader, but in fact the strings are pulled behind the scenes by the colonial occupier.

Ariel Sharon went to Haram Al-Sharif, the Dome of the Rock and the Al-Aqsa mosque in Jerusalem on September 28.[13] *He was es-*

Intifada 2000: The Palestinian Uprising 41

corted by some one thousand Israeli security personnel. The visit of the former Israeli general and cabinet minister is cited as the match that ignited the new Intifada. What does Sharon represent to Palestinians? What does it say about Barak, allowing Sharon to make the visit?

Sharon in Israeli popular mythology is something of a hero. His exploits began in the 1950s. He was responsible for the invasion of the town of Qibia, where they killed about sixty-five innocent people in their homes in retaliation for a raid on an Israeli military patrol in which three soldiers were killed the day before.[14] Thereafter he went from one exploit of this sort to another. He's basically a bully who specializes in the oppression of civilians and enemies who are far less well equipped than he is. He was the pacifier of Gaza after the Israeli occupation of 1967. During the early 1970s he destroyed many homes and relocated Palestinians in order to uproot what the Israelis said were terrorist cells but what in fact were resistance cells inside Gaza. Of course, above all, he was the architect of the invasion of Lebanon in 1982, where he misled his own cabinet into believing that they were going to just go in for a few miles whereas in fact they went into Beirut, killing in the process 17,000 people.[15] He was cited by the Commission of Inquiry into the Events at the Refugee Camps in Beirut (the Kahan commission) as being indirectly responsible for the massacres in the refugee camps of Sabra and Shatila, which were done in an area controlled by the Israelis, although the actual action was perpetrated by Lebanese Maronite militias acting under the supervision of the Israelis.[16]

42 Culture and Resistance

So by any standards at all Ariel Sharon is a war criminal. He's made no secret of the fact that he'd like to drive the rest of the Palestinians out and put them in Jordan. He said the solution of Palestine is what he calls the Jordanian option, to turn Jordan, which is a sovereign country, into a Palestinian state.[17] His appearance on the Al-Aqsa mosque, which is of course held by Israel and has been annexed along with the rest of East Jerusalem since 1967 in full contravention of international law and many UN resolutions, despite the ones vetoed by the United States, was a provocation. The next day, September 29, right after prayers there was a demonstration against his having been there the day before. The Israeli police opened fire on the demonstrators and killed five civilians.[18] As you said, Sharon was there on September 28, with a thousand policemen supplied to him by Barak.

It's quite clear that Barak was behind, or at least approved of, the move. Not so much only as a provocation, I don't know if it was meant to be a provocation to bring forth the horrors that ensued. I don't think his limited brains could foresee this. But I think it was a way of asserting Israeli sovereignty on a sacred Muslim site. It was designed not so much to be provocative as to be offensive, to show that an Israeli military figure who has a long history of brutality and war crimes can appear in one of the holiest places of Islam with impunity. Any Israeli can do that. So that no matter who the Muslims are, their wishes, their feelings, their sense of the sacrosanct can be violated at will by an Israeli. That was the idea. It pitted the ugliest aspects of monotheism against each other. There

Intifada 2000: The Palestinian Uprising

was the Israeli, representative of the Jewish state, trampling all over Muslim places and Islam and in effect saying, We are the military occupier, we can do with you what we wish. And yet none of this was ever reflected in the media. They kept talking about it as a provocation. It wasn't meant as a provocation. It was meant to be an assertion of Israeli and hence Jewish superiority over Islam.

The catechism recited by the likes of Nobel Prize–winner Elie Wiesel, multiple Pulitzer Prize–winner and New York Times *columnist Thomas Friedman, PBS's Charlie Rose, and the Orientalist academic Bernard Lewis is pretty much like this: Camp David collapsed because of Arafat's intransigence and his failure to seize a unique opportunity. The Barak offer went way beyond anything previously proposed. It was a far-reaching and most generous compromise.*

It's simply factually untrue. Before he went, Barak made it absolutely clear that he had no intention of returning to the 1967 borders.[19] That was the principle on which the peace process was started, that there would be a return of all the territory to the June 5, 1967 borders.

Based on UN Security Council Resolution 242.

And UN Security Council Resolution 338. Second, he made it absolutely clear that there would be no return of the refugees. Third, he made it absolutely clear that there would be no return of Jerusalem to Palestinian sovereignty at all. Fourth, he made it also absolutely clear that he had no intention of uprooting the settlements.[20] These are the positions

44   **Culture and Resistance**

on which his whole subsequent negotiation was based. It didn't depart from them. It simply consolidated them. Again, if you look at the facts rather than the suppositions made by the spin doctors of the American and Israeli media, he in fact gave back nothing of East Jerusalem. He didn't concede anything. He simply said, We will allow you a form of sovereignty in the holy places. We will keep the Christian and Armenian sections. You can have a little bit of sovereignty over some of the Muslim holy places, but the real substantive sovereignty over East Jerusalem will remain in Israeli hands. And the vast majority of the city in terms of area would remain under Israel. That was supposed to be a "forward-looking" position. He refused to take in any refugees and took no responsibility for what happened in 1948. This from the leader of a people that has exacted, correctly, reparations for what it endured in the way of anti-Semitism and suffering in World War II. He's telling the Palestinians, We don't even consider your claims. They're simply irrelevant to us. He refused categorically to give up the settlements.

Faced with this, Arafat didn't want to come to a two-week session of this sort, which was not simply to be a continuation of the peace process, but the "final status" negotiation. Arafat couldn't agree. Not only because of the conditions, which were terrible, but also for two other reasons. One is that Arafat was being asked to end the conflict and end any Palestinian claims against Israel and thereby end any Muslim-Christian claims against Israel. He couldn't do it. Secondly, he was also being asked to give up Palestinian

Intifada 2000: The Palestinian Uprising   45

claims to return and self-determination, which again he couldn't do because of simple fear of what would happen to him if he signed on. So, far from it being an opportunity for Arafat to take advantage of Israeli generosity, it was an opportunity for Arafat effectively to commit suicide and to give Israel the last prize, you might say the cherry on the sundae, which was everything they wanted in addition to what Arafat had already conceded, which was 78 percent of what they had in 1948. He also conceded West Jerusalem, which is where I was born and where my family had a house. That was 40 percent Arab. He gave that all away. The concessions Arafat made were vastly more generous and ill-considered than anything the Israelis did. So quite correctly, I think, he rebelled.

Another theme echoed by the pundits is the image of Palestinians as losers. Barak in his Knesset speech on October 30 revived the Abba Eban comment that the Palestinians never miss an opportunity to miss an opportunity.[21]

Israeli information, from the very beginning, has always played on two levels. On one level there's what they call *hasbara*, the Hebrew word for information, which is basically propaganda, for the *goyim*, the foreigners. There is the depiction of Israel as forthcoming, democratic, defensive, victimized, generous, and compassionate. In other words, an image crafted to appeal to the Western liberal conscience. Then on the other hand there's what Israel says to itself and what Barak says to his people. From the very beginning—whether it was Shimon Peres speaking, or Yitzhak Rabin, or Yossi

Beilin, or Ehud Barak, or Benjamin Netanyahu—they all said the same thing. They said, This is a peace process in which we lose nothing. Rabin said it just a few months before Oslo was signed in 1993. He said, I wish Gaza would sink into the sea. It's such a millstone around our necks. It's overpopulated, a million people living under the most miserable conditions. Why should we be responsible? We'll keep the best land and we'll give the rest to the Palestinians.[22]

That's the basis of Oslo. The appeal of the so-called peace camp within the Labor Party has always been that we are going to gain by this. We are going to give up land that's useless. We're going to give up chores that are onerous. Ruling Palestinians. We don't want to do that. Let them do it. We're not going to give up any settlements. Beilin says it all the time. And he is portrayed as the ultimate dove in this country and in Israel. He is always saying, We're not going to give up any of the main settlements. We're going to annex the best land. We're going to keep Jerusalem.[23] You people shouldn't complain, telling the Likud that they had very little reason to object to the arrangements.

If you look carefully at this history, examine it as it is in fact as opposed to the level of *hasbara* or surface propaganda, you realize what, in my opinion, a suicidal game the Israelis are playing. The basis of their politics is that the only argument the Arabs can understand is violence. The occupation is a form of violence, against which throwing of rocks and the occasional terrorist outrage, horrible though they may be, are nothing in comparison to the collective punishment of three

Intifada 2000: The Palestinian Uprising   47

million people which has been going on for the last thirty-three years. Israel is the only country in the world where torture is legally sanctioned. Nearly 20 percent of Israeli citizens in Israel, who happen not to be Jews but Palestinians, are treated essentially as blacks were in South Africa. They are denied rights, not allowed to own, rent, or buy land. Their lands are regularly confiscated. This is a policy of violence and discrimination of the most appalling kind. Obviously, Israel wants to be accepted and recognized. But in fact, its policy of force and occupation and obduracy and unwillingness to listen to the cries of the Palestinians who have been suffering for fifty years have created in Palestinians a resentment that has only increased in time.

It also must be said that Israel signed peace treaties with two Arab countries, Jordan and Egypt, and after twenty years of peace with Egypt relations have remained essentially cold. The Israelis say, We tried. We sent missions. But the Israelis have to face the consequences of their actions. Israel is seen everywhere as responsible for the use of massive weapons, disproportionate violence against civilians, the continued expropriation of land, the building of settlements, the trampling of Palestinian rights. This has made the Arab world and the Islamic world of 300 million Arabs, 1.2 billion Muslims, consider Israel to be a pariah state which has been laying up for itself a sense of resentment and outrage and hostility that cannot go away given the present policy. That's why I say it's suicidal, because in the end Israel is a state in the Middle East. It's not next to Kansas. It's not part of New York. It's 6,000

48   **Culture and Resistance**

miles away. Lebanon is on its northern border. On its eastern border are Syria and Jordan. On its southern border is Egypt. The Palestinians are everywhere inside Israel and on the West Bank and Gaza. You can beat them down, and certainly Israel has the most powerful army. It has a nuclear arsenal of 200 warheads.[24] It has the best air force in the region, and one of the two or three best air forces in the world. Of course it has military and economic superiority. It has above all the support of the United States. But how long can that last? At some point the numbers are going to be against it. I figure that by 2010 there will be an equal number of Palestinians and Israelis on historical Palestine. There will be demographic parity between Jews and Arabs. At which point, how much can the Israelis control? By 2030 there will be twice as many Arabs as there are Jews.[25] So the Jews in Israel will be in a minority.

It's certainly acceptable that they should have political self-determination. But it can't simply be guaranteed by military means. That is not a long-term policy. The only option is peace, and it has to be a real peace between equals as opposed to a peace that it imposed on the weaker party by the stronger one.

You said the Palestinians living in Israel comprise something like 20 percent of the population.

That's correct. A million people.

Intifada 2000: The Palestinian Uprising

In the 1987 uprising they were rather quiescent. However in the 2000 Intifada that has changed dramatically. Why?

One reason is that the treatment of the Palestinian Israelis by the Israeli government historically has been appalling. They were ruled by military edict until 1966. So for eighteen years, from the beginning of the state in 1948, they were an outcast people in their own country. Discriminated against in every conceivable way. They were not allowed to move, to be educated properly, to have certain jobs. In 1966, the military government was lifted and they were given a measure of improved conditions. They were represented in the Knesset. They could vote in elections. They can't own additional land. During that period, from 1966 on, they watched the alienation of their land continue to take place. Many of the villages, like Umm el-Fahm, which was probably the largest Arab village in Israel, lost 10,000 dunams, about 2,500 acres, of its land to the Israeli government.[26] It was simply expropriated for military purposes. They were going to turn it into a target range. As I mentioned, the budget is so little for them. The schools are definitely much less well-endowed. Basic services like electricity and water in the Arab towns and villages are poor.

So there was a massive sense of being discriminated against for the simple reason that they're not Jews. It's a kind of racism that affected the whole community and they finally rose up against it. They saw what the Israeli army was doing in the West Bank and Gaza, and they identified with the Palestinians there. That's the second most important thing. What

50　　　　　　**Culture and Resistance**

the Israelis have tried to do has been to destroy the sense of unity of these people, who are divided by geography. The Palestinians of Israel are Israeli citizens. People in the West Bank used to be Jordanians. In Gaza they were stateless people who used to be under Egyptian rule. They're now in an indeterminate state. The Palestinians in Lebanon are stateless people. One of the most important achievements of the PLO historically was to make the Palestinian people feel as one people. I think the whole of the policy of the United States and Israel in the last twenty years has been to keep digging away at Palestinian identity, to fragment it, so that people don't feel that they are part of the same entity which has suffered collectively as a people under the Israelis who have behind them of course the United States.

All these calculations turned out to be wrong. There was an immediate sense of identification that the lot of Palestinians under military occupation in the West Bank and Gaza dramatically resembled the lot of Palestinians who were Israeli citizens who were denied the same things and were in fact severely oppressed and handicapped and disadvantaged. They also rose up in demonstrations against the Israelis. What they got was an Israeli military response. They didn't get a political response, with the result that thirteen citizens of Israel were killed by the police of Israel.[27]

So there's also a continuity of policy of Israelis toward Palestinians, that they're not to be treated as a people. Behind this policy is an irrational fear of excavating the past, because if you allow the past to be looked at frankly and openly, as

Intifada 2000: The Palestinian Uprising 51

many of us have been advocating, Israelis and Palestinians, you will see what Israel's original sin is, that it destroyed Palestine in 1948. And that, far from going away, this original sin has been returning in one form after another. It has widened its scope to take in not only the West Bank and Gaza, not only Palestinians in the diaspora—the people who created the PLO were not residents of the West Bank and Gaza, they were in Kuwait and Lebanon—not only the Palestinian citizens, but all of them acting together. They have reaffirmed the existence of a denied Palestinian aspiration for self-determination and the need for reparation from Israel, which is the cause of most of their woes.

It's a major problem for which, alas, neither the Israeli nor the American leadership is adequate. The problem is thought of in janitorial terms. Move them around a little bit, give them a little bit of something. Allow them to drive in the same cars with us and maybe ride in the same bus, that kind of thing, but no substantial improvement and no realization of their national claims. And that hasn't worked. In fact, the claims have grown stronger and the need has grown stronger. And the Israeli denials have grown more shrill and strident and more out of touch with reality. For any Israeli, the primary thing to do now is to confront the problem within their own borders, confront this large group of citizens who simply on the basis of religion are treated as second-rate.

Israel is unique in many ways. It is a state that has no constitution. It's government by a set of basic laws. It makes very radical distinctions between Jews and non-Jews, right down to the statistical abstracts. Everything is governed by who's a Jew and who isn't. This is unworkable. It's a state that's run effectively by religious authority. Many citizens of Israel are genuinely worried about the fate of secular Jews who will not accept being ruled by orthodox and conservative clerics. Rather than confront this in an open way, there is this return to the traditional response of the Israelis, either to deny or to reaffirm something completely different that has very little to do with reality. The Palestinians bear a great responsibility—Palestinian intellectuals certainly, but even Palestinian citizens and other Arabs—to make this known in a peaceful way, to Israelis, and to say, We are here, you are here. You can't deny, you can't repress forever. You have to seek out the truth in your past, the truth in ours. Maybe through a truth and reconciliation commission such as the one that took place in South Africa.

What's stunning about this conflict is that, for fifty years, these two communities have been working on totally opposed principles. The Israelis have said, We have a right to this land. There was nobody here. In one way or another they've been saying this all along. It doesn't matter what happened in 1948. Let's try to deal with 1967. Those are unacceptable responses in the twenty-first century. It behooves everyone to say, This is simply unacceptable behavior. You can't simply wipe the slate clean to suit yourself and your policy. You have to face the other party and try to take responsibility for what you did, the way everybody has. The Japanese have taken responsibility for what they did to the Koreans.

Intifada 2000: The Palestinian Uprising   53

The Germans for the Jews. The Poles for the Jews. In this the Israelis are not different from these people. What they've done has imposed on another people a calamity which continues to this very day, along with all the denials. No, they weren't here. This was an empty land. God gave it to us. These are just Arabs. They don't count. These arguments are still being used today. Or, basically, These are second-class people, barbarians. We are much more developed. That in my opinion is the problem today. It cannot be addressed by the ridiculous peace process imposed by the whims of the United States and the Israeli leadership.

After the Balfour Declaration, Chaim Weizmann, when asked about the indigenous population of Palestine said that, "there are a few hundred thousand Negroes, but that is a matter of no significance."[28]

I don't know about that, but that's been the attitude. It doesn't really matter. And if need be, as Theodor Herzl said, they'll have to be "spirited" away.[29] Look at the arguments within the Zionist movement, all of which are public. There's nothing arcane or secret or esoteric about it. It's in the Zionist archives from the 1940s, as studied by Palestinian and Israeli scholars. It's quite clear that the Palestinians' sheer physical presence has always been the main problem. Whether it's trying to get rid of them or pretend that they weren't there or they're really not the original inhabitants or something else, all of this is what I'd call gratuitous epistemological willfulness to pretend that the Palestinians are a negligible quantity. The problem is increasing. It hasn't decreased.

54　　　**Culture and Resistance**

Settlers and Orthodox Israeli Jews have staged demonstrations and protests and thrown rocks at cars and buses. Have there been any instances of Israeli security forces opening fire on them?

None at all. Let me give you a very dramatic example. The town of Hebron is essentially an Arab town. There were no Jews in it before 1967. After 1967, they managed to establish by force a colony of somewhere between 300 and 400 Jews inside a town that contains roughly 120,000 to 130,000 Arabs. Those settlers, who constitute roughly three-tenths of a percent of the population, now control 20 percent of the town by virtue of the peace process.[30] The part of the town that they occupy is right in the middle of the Arab territory, not on the outskirts. So they can walk through the town surrounded by army personnel who protect them and who also provide them with weapons. They are there on a daily, an hourly basis, to demonstrate their rights as Jews in an Arab town to override the wishes of the overwhelming majority of the citizens, who are Arabs. And it's this group that produced Baruch Goldstein, who murdered twenty-nine worshipers in the mosque in Hebron, which is also held by the Israelis.[31] When I visited in 1992, I was astonished. In order to get into the mosque, which also contains a yeshiva, you have to pass through Israeli barricades and metal detectors and a group of soldiers sitting at the door of the mosque with their feet up on the table, which is a very provocative thing in an Islamic context, and their boots stuck in the faces of the worshipers trying to go through. It's through this barricade that Baruch

Intifada 2000: The Palestinian Uprising

Goldstein passed in February 1994 and opened fire on the worshipers.

This is the current situation multiplied hundreds of times in the West Bank and Gaza, where the settlers are rampaging vigilantes. Settlements are built next to Arab towns. They have arms. They are protected by the soldiers. They also are soldiers themselves. Goldstein was a member of the Israeli military reserve. They go out and prey on these Arab villages and terrorize them. They break their windows, burn their cars, destroy their crops. The settlers are a tremendous provocation. The problem is that they've been increasing under Barak, who came to power in July 1999. He increased the number of settlements more than under Netanyahu and certainly more than under Peres and Rabin. So the settlement problem is a real one because it means taking land away and adding intrusive, illegal Israeli nationals to what is in effect a Palestinian territory. This is one of the basic flaws of the peace process, that while it's going forward and the Palestinians are signing away, the Israelis are making it harder for there to be a viable Palestinian state. They are in all the territories. They control the Jordan Valley. So that there will be no border between a Palestinian state and any other Arab state. All the borders will be controlled by the Israelis through settlements and military outposts.

You wrote a series of three articles in Al-Ahram Weekly *entitled "American Zionism."*[32] *In the lead article you discuss an interview you*

56   **Culture and Resistance**

had with Avi Shavit of Ha'aretz, a major Israeli newspaper. You drew certain conclusions from that interaction.

The distinction I was trying to draw was that the Israel position is that the Palestinians are there, but they are a lesser people. The right wing says, We conquered them and they have to be our servants. The left wing says, We can rearrange them in some inoffensive way. Today, because the Israelis live there and they see Palestinians every minute of the day, as their servants and waiters in the restaurants of Tel Aviv or their chauffeurs and taxi drivers, all those people who work in the Occupied Territories and in Jerusalem, they know they're there as a physical presence. So that's the Israeli Zionist awareness, consciousness of Palestinians. The American Zionist by contrast really doesn't think of the Palestinians as a real thing at all. There's a kind of fantasy element in which Palestinians are a gratuitous ideological fiction created to harass the Israelis and therefore act as avatars of anti-Semitism. That's what Bernard Lewis keeps saying all the time, this is Arab anti-Semitism. Detaching the Palestinians from their history, from the fact that they were supplanted and their society destroyed in 1948 and have been under military occupation since 1967, American Zionism is much more dangerous than Israeli Zionism. It's based on a fantasy, that the Palestinians are really not there at all and can be treated as microbes in some way or at best as an ideological fiction.

Intifada 2000: The Palestinian Uprising   57

The interview was given a prominent place.

It appeared on the front page of *Ha'aretz*, in the Friday supplement.[33] Obviously Shavit's views and mine are quite different, but at least he was willing to listen to me. This interview could never have appeared in an American newspaper. They would never have dared to run such a thing. Simply because the whole subject of Palestine is virtually forbidden in the United States and can only be treated as a subsidiary of a subsidiary of a subsidiary. This is the principle upon which many of the Jewish organizations function.

A couple of years ago you made a documentary film for the BBC called In Search of Palestine.[34] *After being shown on BBC2 and then on BBC World, it has more or less disappeared. The BBC was almost totally unsuccessful in getting it on U.S. television. Why was that?*

There's a history of films from a Palestinian point of view in this country. There's an organized response from the Zionist organizations to try to stop it, try to block it. They try to argue it down. They try to make sure that the advertisers of the program, if it's on television, pay a very heavy price for it in withdrawn support. If they want to show one Palestinian film they have to show five films from the Israeli point of view. What happened to my film was very much of that order. Nobody would take it. The BBC couldn't place it in this country. Finally, through personal connections, I was able to get Channel 13 in New York, PBS, to show it once, and I think it was shown on public television in San Francisco, also

58　　　　　　　**Culture and Resistance**

once. Effectively, the film has disappeared. The notion is that the representation of Palestinians as human beings with a history and a cause is simply forbidden.

As an example, during the last six weeks of the Al-Aqsa Intifada that began in late September, the *New York Times* on its op-ed page has run only three pro-Palestinian articles, one by an Israeli who argued the Palestinian case, another by a Jordanian, and a third, a very strong article, by Allegra Pacheco, an Israeli lawyer who was in the United States at the time.[35] The rest have all been pro-Israeli. That's been true of the *Washington Post*, of all the major papers. In all the reporting no maps have been shown, so you can't really tell what the Palestinians have lost and where they are confined, in little bantustans in the West Bank and Gaza.

The net result is that the picture of Palestine and Palestinians that circulates in the popular consciousness is very limited. Mercifully, there are alternative sources. Your program, Alternative Radio, is obviously one. The Internet brings extracts from the Israeli press, the British press, the Arab press, from independent and alternative journalists writing all over the world. These are available in cyberspace. But the overwhelming official consensus is that Israel is a besieged, victimized country. The Arabs will not accept it because they are anti-Semitic.

It should also be said that the Arab world itself is in a very bad state. All of the rulers without exception are tyrannical and anti-democratic. There is no democracy. The Arabs are paying the heaviest price for this. It's not being paid for by the

Intifada 2000: The Palestinian Uprising 59

United States. It's being paid for by Arabs, whose general situation—whether health or education or general income levels or infrastructure or transportation or environment—has steadily decreased in the last few years, never more precipitously than in the years since the peace process began in the early 1990s. So I think that explains why Palestine has become a kind of touchstone for Arab opinion everywhere. It represents the injustice of the ruler towards the ruled, whether it's Israelis ruling Palestinians or Palestinians ruling Palestinians, using the Palestinian Authority against Palestinian citizens in territories occupied by Israel or people rebelling against unjust authority and delegitimized regimes in Morocco or Egypt, all of which are supported by the United States. So it's not surprising that what we have is, I think, a major turning point in the history of the modern Middle East.

What can be done to reverse what you call the unhealthy quality of public discourse in the Arab world?

One has to begin first by mobilizing the community of supporters in this country, of which there are many, for the rights of the Palestinians and the genuine course toward peace and reconciliation between Palestinians, Arabs generally, and Israelis. So we need to mobilize opinion here. We must have more pressure, because the polls that I've seen since the early 1970s all have shown that American popular consensus is way ahead of official policy. The role of the political action committees and the Israeli lobby and the media have been inordinately reductionist and have taken positions

60   **Culture and Resistance**

far in arrears to that of most Americans, who, when given a quarter of a chance, will see the justice and the injustice of the situation. The constant monitoring of the media to show the imbalances, as some are beginning to do all over the country, is important. NPR and the TV networks and newspapers, like the *New York Times*, should be bombarded constantly with alternatives and letters and organized campaigns to change their coverage.

Second, the most important thing is to delegitimize the Israeli military occupation—it has gone on, as I said, for thirty-three years—just as the anti-apartheid activism in this country made it impossible for apartheid to function by organizing on a mass basis. Israel is the largest recipient of foreign aid in the history of this country. There is a constant exchange between American academics and Israeli universities. I myself have urged people who go to Israel, invited by one or another university, to make a point to go to Palestinian universities. We have to do this work ourselves, to include the larger community of academics, writers, artisans, intellectuals, peace activists, anti-imperialists, anti-discrimination activists, of whom there are many in this country. The civil rights movement. The African American movement. The antiwar movement. The women's movement. To engage in this and see that it's part of a common struggle.

The United States sells tens of billions of dollars in arms to the Middle East, whether it's the Gulf countries or Israel.[36] They're some of the largest purchasers of arms in the world. What we have to do is to take the curtain away so that the de-

Intifada 2000: The Palestinian Uprising 61

bate about the Middle East is not hobbled by the fear of inciting the Zionist lobby. Just because the *New Republic* or *Commentary* go after somebody doesn't mean that they should stop. One shouldn't be afraid of what is a paper tiger. They have very thin support. They're more noisy than they are right in what they do.

It's a challenge that can be met if young people are mobilized and have a critical awareness of what's going on. There's no excuse for not knowing.

There's been a lot of media focus on Palestinian sectarian formations such as Hamas and Islamic Jihad. What's going on in civil society?

There's been a widening gap between the rich and the poor in Middle East society. Globalization, with its transformation of economies into vast consumer markets for venture capitalism, has made things worse. There are small isolated sectors connected to the regimes that are enriching themselves. The vast mass of people live in poverty with threats of eviction, the inability to find jobs or feed their children and send them to school. I think it's wrong to see the Islamic organizations simply as terrorist formations. They certainly have provided a civic alternative to the governments, which are all, without exception, corrupt. Their budgets have been given up to enormous schemes. The Palestinian budget, for example, has almost nothing for infrastructure, but enormous sums for the bureaucracy. That's the kind of lopsided distortions you have. People go to the mosques and the religious schools for the kind of sustenance

Culture and Resistance

they can't get elsewhere. Militarily, the militants of Hamas and Islamic Jihad have really been unsuccessful. They've also demonstrated that they don't really have a message beyond the kind of sustenance I was talking about.

In other words, for the last twenty years, since the emergence of Hamas—but this is also true of the Muslim Brotherhood in Egypt and the Islamic Salvation Front in Algeria—the message is not getting through to the people, simply because they don't have a message about the future. You can't simply say Islam is the only solution. You have to deal with problems of electricity, water, the environment, transportation. Those can't be Islamic. So they've failed on that level. I think it's a complex formation that suggests that secularism is the dominant force. Islam remains the last cultural bastion to defend against the intrusions and the aggressions on the Arab Muslim by Israel and the United States and the regimes. So I would say it's a symbol of resistance rather than something that can immediately be translated into a political message or a political vision for the future. It isn't. That has to come from citizens who think in terms of coexistence, of cooperation, of, let's say in the Arab world, a common Arab market, a common pooling of Arab resources, a common policy on immigration and integration of a kind, alas, that hasn't been the case for at least two generations.

Intifada 2000: The Palestinian Uprising   63

In light of the 2000 Intifada, what does that mean for your proposal of last year for a binational state where Palestinians and Israelis would live in one country?[37]

The preeminent thing now is the end of military occupation. The realities on the ground, in fact, bear out what I've been saying. The Palestinians and the Israelis are so integrated, the territory is so small that you can't have a situation in which one population imposes itself militarily upon another. I'm very much against evictions and driving people off. This is what happened to us. I do think, however, that the settlements have to be dismantled and the populations have to face each other as not only neighbors but in fact in coexistence, in one basically homogenous state, which we call historical Palestine, whether you call it Israel or a Palestinian state. The economies and the histories are so intertwined that I still think that in the end a binational state is the only long-term solution.

I suppose in the interim, as a kind of transition, one would have to have two states both free of military occupation. Then, out of that freedom, the Palestinian state could pursue policies that unite it not just with Israel but with Jordan, Lebanon, and the other countries that make up this very densely populated and potentially integrated part of the world. The point is that partition, separation, has not worked. It has always meant that one side of the partition is disadvantaged and the other is the outsider and more powerful. This produces more problems. Since the 1940s, when most of the

64   Culture and Resistance

Arab states got their independence and Israel was created, the problems have multiplied. They haven't gone away. Coexistence behind barbed wire, behind suspicion and violence, state violence of the kind that Israel wages, and the kind that the Syrian regime has waged, for example, and the Iraqi regime has waged, simply doesn't produce the kind of stability and peaceful coexistence that everyone desires.

I still think a binational state is the optimal solution and will come. But, alas, a lot of time has to pass and some of these tremendous vestiges of the past have to be worked through.

How are you doing?

I'm OK. I have a chronic illness which can't be cured but can be held at bay. Periodically I have to have treatment. One loses somewhat as one ages, but the idea is to keep going.

It's a rather ironic situation in terms of your health that you're treated at Long Island Jewish hospital by an eminent Indian doctor who is surrounded by Irish nurses.

And an American Indian assistant. And I'm a Palestinian patient. It's lovely. I feel like a privileged person. I consider myself the longest serving inmate of that particular institution, having been in treatment for seven or eight years. They are very kind to me. I love being in their hands. I don't like being there. I wish I wasn't. But if one has to be there, that's a very good place to be.

Intifada 2000: The Palestinian Uprising

So unlike the title of your memoir, Out of Place, *do you feel a bit at ease?*

No, I still feel out of place, but there are degrees of out of placeness, and this is, considering the contradiction of living in New York, a very tolerable one.

What books do you have coming up?

I have a large collection of essays called *Reflections on Exile,* which is about to appear. Harvard is publishing it. Then I have a book of interviews called *Culture, Politics, and Power,* which Pantheon is bringing out next fall. Then I have two small books, one on opera and one on humanism. They are both based on lectures. The opera book is based on talks I gave at Cambridge. The one on humanism is from lectures I gave at Columbia.

Do you have time to pursue your avocation of music?

I'm doing a book of conversations with my friend, the pianist and conductor Daniel Barenboim.[38] It will be completed by the end of this year. As much as I can, I play piano and chamber music with friends.

Notes

1. See Benny Morris, *The Birth of the Palestinian Refugee Problem 1947–1949* (Cambridge: Cambridge University Press, 1989), among others.

2. For complete tables and statistics on Palestinian refugees, see the website and reports of the United Nations Relief and Works Agency

66   **Culture and Resistance**

for Palestine Refugees in the Near East (UNRWA): http://www.un.org/unrwa/.

3   See Naseer H. Aruri, ed., *Palestinian Refugees: The Right of Return* (London: Pluto Books, 2001).

4   For detailed reports on the settlements, see the website of the Foundation for Middle East Peace (FMEP) and its newsletter *The Report on Israeli Settlement in the Occupied Territories,* which is available online at http://www.fmep.org/.

5   For detailed data on injuries and deaths in the Al-Aqsa Intifada, see the websites of B'Tselem (The Israeli Information Center for Human Rights in the Occupied Territories) and the Palestinian Red Crescent Society at http://www.btselem.org/English/Statistics/Al_Aqsa_Fatalities_Tables.asp and http://www.palestinercs.org/crisistables/oct_2000_table.htm.

6   David R. Francis, "Economist Tallies Swelling Cost of Israel to US," *Christian Science Monitor,* December 9, 2002, p. 16. Official U.S. aid since 1973, calculated in 2001 dollars.

7   See Stephen Zunes, "UN Resolutions Being Violated by Countries other than Iraq," Foreign Policy in Focus, October 3, 2002. Available online at http://www.fpif.org/.

8   "The Spreading of Palestine's War," *The Economist* (U.S. Edition), October 28, 2000.

9   See Samih K. Farsoun and Christina E. Zacharia, *Palestine and the Palestinians* (Boulder: Westview Press, 1997), pp. 123–25.

10   See The Palestinian Academic Society for the Study of International Affairs (PASSIA), *The Palestinian Question in Maps: 1878–2002* (Jerusalem: PASSIA, 2002), Maps 40–48 (pp. 110–27).

11   See the website of The Foundation for Middle East Peace (http://www.fmep.org/reports/).

12   See, among other sources, Norman Finkelstein, *Image and Reality of the Israel-Palestine Conflict,* updated ed. (New York: Verso, 2003) and Noam Chomsky, *Middle East Illusions* (Boulder: Rowman and Littlefield, 2003).

Intifada 2000: The Palestinian Uprising 67

13 See Robert Fisk, "Bloodbath at the Dome of the Rock," *The Independent* (London), September 30, 2000, p. 1.

14 See Emma Brokes, "The Bulldozer: These are Busy Times for Ariel Sharon," *The Guardian* (London), November 7, 2001, p. 2.

15 Robert Fisk, "This is a Place of Filth and Blood Which Will Forever Be Associated with Sharon," *The Independent* (London), February 6, 2001, p. 1. See also Robert Fisk, *Pity the Nation: The Abduction of Lebanon*, updated ed. (New York: Nation Books, 2002).

16 See Julie Flint, "The Sharon Files," *The Guardian* (London), November 28, 2001, p. 6.

17 Nicole Gaouette, "Deep Splits Face Israel's New Leader," *Christian Science Monitor,* February 7, 2001, p. 1.

18 Ross Dunn, "Muslims Shot in Clash at Jerusalem Site," *The Times* (London), September 30, 2000.

19 See Naseer H. Aruri, *Dishonest Broker: The U.S. Role in Israel and Palestine* (Cambridge: South End Press, 2003), chapter 10. See also Tanya Reinhart, *Israel/Palestine: How to End the War of 1948* (New York: Seven Stories Press, 2002).

20 Aruri, *Dishonest Broker*, chapter 20.

21 Barak quoted in Lee Hockstader, "Israeli Helicopters Hit Key Palestinian Offices," *Washington Post,* October 31, 2000, p. A1.

22 Clyde Haberman, "Yitzhak Rabin: Pragmatist Leading Israelis From Isolation to New Peace," *New York Times,* September 12, 1993, p. 1: 12; Sarah Helm, "Talks Reveal a Glimmer of Hope on Golan," *The Independent* (London), September 4, 1992, p. 9.

23 David Zev Harris and Margot Dudkevitch, "Settler Leaders Upbeat after 'Positive' Meeting with Beilin," *Jerusalem Post,* February 11, 2000, p. 4A.

24 See Seymour M. Hersh, *The Samson Option: Israel's Nuclear Arsenal and American Foreign Policy* (New York: Random House, 1991); Avner Cohen, *Israel and the Bomb* (New York: Columbia University Press, 1998); BBC World News, "Israel 'May Have 200 Nuclear

68   **Culture and Resistance**

Weapons,'" August, 23, 2000. Report avaiilable online at http://news.bbc.co.uk/1/hi/world/middle_east/892941.stm.

25 Harvey Morris, "Demography Drives Debate in Israel Over Settlements," *Financial Times* (London), June 14, 2002, p. 11.

26 See "MKs Almost Come to Blows over Umm el-Fahm," *Jerusalem Post,* October 21, 1998, p. 4.

27 Sharon Waxman, "Israeli Jews and Arabs Find Common Ground at 'Peace Tents,'" *Washington Post,* October 18, 2000, p. A23.

28 See quotations in Noam Chomsky, *Deterring Democracy,* updated ed. (New York: Hill and Wang, 1992), pp. 434–35.

29 See Nur Masalha, *Expulsion of the Palestinians: The Concept of "Transfer" in Zionist Political Thought, 1882–1948* (Washington, D.C.: Institute for Palestine Studies, 1992), p. 9.

30 See Ian Fisher, "In Grief, Israeli Family Questions Army Aid to Settlers," *New York Times,* December 18, 2002, p. A10. See also PASSIA, *Palestine Question in Maps,* Map 29 (pp. 78–79).

31 Chris Hedges, "Soldier Fired at Crowd, Survivors of Massacre Say," *New York Times,* March 16, 1994, p. A1.

32 Edward W. Said, "American Zionism—The Real Problem," three parts, *Al-Ahram Weekly* 500 (September 21–27, 2000), 502 (October 5–11, 2000), 506 (November 2–8, 2000). Online at http://www.ahram.org.eg/weekly/.

33 Ari Shavit, "My Right of Return," *Ha'aretz,* August 18, 2000.

34 *In Search of Palestine: A Documentary Film Narrated by Edward Said* (London: BBC, 1998).

35 Rami G. Khouri, "Israel's Deadly Errors," *New York Times,* October 10, 2000, p. A27; Allegra Pacheco, "Palestinians in a State of Siege," *New York Times,* March 16, 2001, p. A19; Amira Hass, "Separate and Unequal on the West Bank," *New York Times,* September 2, 2001, p. 4: 9.

36 Richard F. Grimmett, *Conventional Arms Transfers to Developing Nations, 1994 to 2001,* August 6, 2002 (RL31529) (Washington, D.C.:

Congressional Research Service, 2002). See also Gideon Burrows, *The No-Nonsense Guide to the Arms Trade* (London: Verso, 2002).

37   Edward W. Said, "The One-State Solution," *New York Times Magazine,* January 10, 1999, p. 6: 36–39.

38   Daniel Barenboim and Edward W. Said, *Parallels and Paradoxes: Explorations in Music and Society* (New York: Pantheon, 2002).

What They Want Is My Silence

Santa Fe, New Mexico, May 2, 2001

Since the Al-Aqsa Intifada began in late September, a number of events have occurred, including the election of Ariel Sharon as Prime Minister of Israel. What's your assessment of the current situation on the ground in Palestine?

It's stalemated. I don't think there's any clear direction, except on both sides there's a return to earlier, almost primordial positions for the Palestinians to stay on the land and to resist to the best of their ability and for the Israelis to get them off the land. That's Sharon's policy. The policy is to use what they call "restraint" but what in fact is disproportionate force, including helicopter gunships, missiles, and tanks, against a basically unarmed and defenseless civilian population and to do it out of a position of total asymmetry that is often obscured by the media. This isn't a battle between two states. It's a battle in which a state with basically a colonial army is attacking a colonized stateless population using all

72   **Culture and Resistance**

forms of collective punishment. Politically, there really isn't any way forward. What the Israelis want is the status quo without Palestinian resistance and what the Palestinians want is, officially, at least, the resumption of negotiations to the point that was reached in the last days of the Clinton administration. But for the people, what they want is the end of Israeli occupation.

Have the Palestinians done a better job in telling their story, getting their narrative out?

I don't think so, simply because the weight of Israeli power is so great that the Palestinians don't have a chance. There is no organization. There are a few websites that if you want you can go to and get up-to-date Palestinian information on what's happening. But in the sense that there's a narrative, that there are maps that show that what is at stake is military and settlement occupation versus liberation, none of that is easily available. The leading papers constantly refer to "Palestinian violence," which seems to be gratuitous and directed at Jews. A massive propaganda effort on the part of Israel, which has employed public relations firms in the United States, has the entire U.S. Congress at its beck and call, and has an enormous amount of financial, political, and other resources blocking any effort at the UN to protect Palestinian civilians against Israeli military onslaught.[1] So the net result is that there is a very skewed situation in which Palestinians are dying. There are now over 400 dead and upwards of 14,000

What They Want Is My Silence   73

seriously injured, with little political benefit.[2] It's a tragic and absolutely unacceptable situation.

The Al-Aqsa Intifada now has been largely relegated to the back pages of the newspapers. For example, today, the Albuquerque Journal *has a small item on page 4. The* New York Times *has a piece on page 11.[3] And the local Santa Fe paper,* The New Mexican, *has nothing at all. Unless there is some major atrocity or conflagration, it's largely low-level background noise now.*

My impression is that that is very much the popular Israeli feeling, that the Arabs are a nuisance and their presence is a fly in the ointment. Daily life for most Israelis in places like Tel Aviv and Haifa and Hertzlia goes on. They're completely insulated from what is taking place. Even the settlers on the West Bank and Gaza don't have to see or deal with Palestinians. They're protected from them, just as whites were protected from blacks during apartheid because of the homeland system and because the roads went around in such a way as to avoid the sight, in that case, of blacks. There's constant encroachment, besiegement. There is the economic suffocation of the Palestinians taking place. No one's recording that. It can't be recorded by conventional means. Then the Israelis are trying to project an image of beleaguered victimhood, that this is a continuation of what Hitler did to the Jews, the most unscrupulous kind of propaganda, basically blaming the victims.

74   Culture and Resistance

In today's New York Times, *there is a full-page ad from the American Jewish Committee rehearsing some of the shibboleths surrounding the conflict.*[4] *How can the Palestinians make their case heard in the face of such publicity?*

The ads are terrible things because they're basically lies, not just lies, but they remove entirely the context. They quote passages from the Egyptian and Syrian press, something that a mufti may have said, without supplying the context, which is that Palestinians are under attack by a Jewish state that is doing what it does in the name of the Jewish people and therefore there's a causal relationship between the resentment and hatred that people feel in the Arab and Islamic world toward the Jews, not because of classic European anti-Semitism, but because of what Israel is doing, which is barbaric. There's no other word for it.

Second, what the ads don't show is the vast outpouring of racist sentiment on the part of Jews. A few days ago, the main rabbi of the Shas Party, Ovadia Yosef, said that the Palestinians should be exterminated. They're snakes, they should be killed.[5] If you were to cull the Israeli press, you'd find far worse sentiments expressed about Arabs and Muslims and Palestinians than in this silly collection of random sayings, most of them probably manufactured by the American Jewish Committee for the American consumer, who doesn't know. Americans have no idea what their money is financing. All of this is paid for by the United States. The oppression of Palestinians is funded by the $5 billion that as American tax-

What They Want Is My Silence

payers we are giving Israel without any strings attached, as well as the power to use arms that are meant for defensive purposes for offensive purposes.

In the meantime, Palestinians, unfortunately, haven't yet come to the awareness that what we need is an organized campaign, which I think can be done. There's a large Palestinian diaspora community that hasn't been mobilized. There are many resources in Palestine, in the Arab world, which haven't been mobilized. We're still at a very primitive level of fighting for turf, over who's going to lead what. We're still under the thumb of a tyrannical and, in my opinion, at this point, useless, Palestinian Authority that wants to try to control the information so as to keep itself in power and to go back to negotiations that nobody wants. Certainly most Palestinians don't want to return to negotiations for an interim settlement that gives the Israelis the right to continue the settlements, which have been escalating under Barak. Most people think that Barak was a generous, nice man who was defeated because he was too soft on the Palestinians. The fact is that he was as brutal as Sharon. The rate of settlement under his regime was greater than that under the four or five previous prime ministers.

So this is a continuation of a policy that has been unremittingly active in oppressing and subduing Palestinians in methods that far outstrip anything that was done in South Africa under apartheid. This needs to be pointed out, and it hasn't been because the Palestinian leadership and many of the elite still believe that the way to do it is to try to

76   **Culture and Resistance**

get the attention of the American administration, which is heedless. If you look at what Colin Powell said when he asked that the Israelis withdraw from Gaza when they made that famous incursion around the middle of April, he was basically blaming the Palestinians for provoking them. The Bush administration, like all American administrations, is hostile to Palestinian aspirations. Therefore, we should concentrate on constituencies in the United States that are friendly to us, the universities, the churches, the African American community, the Latino community, the women's community. We've simply neglected them.

What's at the root of that neglect? Why hasn't there been more outreach?

Probably the root is the sense of terrible desperation and encirclement. There's no way of overestimating the pressure that all Palestinians feel. Here we are, being killed by a ruthless enemy, and all we have in our defense are young men throwing stones at tanks and missiles and helicopter gunships. That is the basic reality. We have a leadership that is unable to lead, for whatever reason. For one, the leadership is in prison. Arafat has been caged up in Ramallah for a number of months. The Israelis have in effect locked him up in a cell and thrown away the key.[6] He can't get to Gaza. There's a policy of extrajudicial assassination whereby leaders are picked off so that everybody who occupies a leadership position in the Palestinian community is threatened directly by Israel with murder and assassination. Most people are having a

What They Want Is My Silence

terrible time economically, finding it hard to put food on the table for their children. Most people are unable to work. There's more than 50 percent unemployment.[7] There's a sense in which we are alone. We are surrounded. The world is paying us no attention, after a hundred years of struggle against this determined enemy. That's the main reason.

The other reason is ignorance. The Palestinian elites, intellectuals and others, still think that there's a shortcut to influencing America, which is the main actor in this besides Israel. Without America, none of this could be done. There's an ignorance of how this country works and what the points of pressure might be. Wherever these pressure points have been used, they've worked. For example, during the year 2000 there was a successful effort to stop Ben & Jerry's ice cream from using water taken from Israeli settlements on the Golan Heights.[8] So Ben & Jerry's became the focus of pressure and boycott, and in the end they stopped. These tactics in fact work. But what you need is a new leadership, an alternative leadership of intellectuals who make that kind of action a principal focus and don't get diverted by things like worrying about the Arab League or whether the British or the Germans are going to do something. What we need is a disciplined focus on the main actors. One is Israel and the Israeli people, who have to be addressed. We've never done that. The second is America and the American people, at least those sectors of this gigantic country that might join us in a battle against this unending war.

78 Culture and Resistance

To what extent do you think the Arabs themselves have been colonized, particularly in the United States?

The Arabs in the United States are a relatively new community. They are recent arrivals mostly, unintegrated, politically unsophisticated communities whose point of reference remains their own countries. The Syrian community looks to Syria, the Egyptians to Egypt, the Lebanese to Lebanon. Many of the same problems that they grew up with in the Middle East are here. Some Lebanese don't trust other Lebanese, replicating the sectarian animosities of Lebanon. Lebanese and Syrians are not close. Lebanese and Palestinians are not close. So there's that problem. It's not exactly being colonized. They are in a situation that is unfamiliar and uncertain, so they can't act as empowered citizens because they are too busy trying to become integrated and become citizens. It's the generation after that, the generation of my children, which I think is very politically aware. And they're slowly organizing. But it takes time.

The Jews were not organized until roughly after 1967, and that was because Israel was victorious and there was an attempt to capitalize on that. We come from a background of tremendous military, political, and territorial losses. That's very hard to reverse. We have a sense of defeat and failure in our psychological armature which has to be overcome. That's why it's important to learn the lessons in the wider society of the United States and liberation movements around the world. We haven't taken advantage of

What They Want Is My Silence 79

that. There's a lot of goodwill and a lot of people are willing to help us.

Do you think that the fear that's present in your generation is somewhat less in the younger generation?

There's no question about it. There's also a lot of understandable contempt for what my generation has wrought. All you have to do is look at the panorama in the Arab world. The problem is, and I've found this in working with young people in some of the new Arab organizations, that because of this contempt, they haven't been able to draw from my generation the experiences and the accumulation of knowledge and achievements that we've made. These new organizations are reinventing the wheel, starting from scratch. They're going back and doing things that have already been done and don't need to be done again and can be built on rather than ignored and contemptuously swept aside. It's a problem of generational continuity which has to be worked out. I think it is being worked out.

Although we're vastly outnumbered and don't have the resources of the Jewish community or many of the other ethnic communities in this country, there is a tremendous reservoir of competence and achievement among young people which I see every time I go to universities around the country. There are young Arab Americans allied with African Americans, women, Native Americans, who are very sophisticated. What we need now is an apparatus, a rethinking of how all of them can work together.

80   Culture and Resistance

You just gave a talk in Bellingham at Western Washington University. What was the reception like there? I ask that because it's not quite akin to Berkeley, Madison, or Boulder.

I gave a major lecture on humanism which didn't deal with Palestine. But earlier in the day I talked to a group of about fifty or sixty students from anthropology, literature, political science. I found a startling, I wouldn't say unanimity, but openness and not only openness but acceptance of the Palestinian position. There were no Arab Americans. The students were mostly from the Northwest. They had a very good understanding of the Palestinian situation, of the political situation in the Middle East, and the work of the Zionist lobby in this country. Even more ironically, one of their professors, one of the leading professors at that university, happens to be an American Jew who is not a Zionist. Thanks to his teaching and the readings that he assigns from my books, Noam Chomsky's books, and those of others, these kids have come around. That's a perfect example.

A few weeks before I was at Princeton. I've been giving a lot of lectures at universities. The minority is seen as right-wing extremist Zionists. The rest are very open and compassionate. I was in London last week. I gave a talk. There must have been more than 2,000 people there, a lot of them Arab, but a lot of them English. I also spoke at the School of Oriental and African Studies. Hundreds of students turned up from all over the Third World. There, too, what startled me was the amazing openness and willingness

What They Want Is My Silence 81

to listen to the Palestinian position. We've never tapped that in any systematic way. That's what strikes me as so stupid on the part of the conventional Arafatist leadership.

So I try my best to draw some of that off to focus it on helping Palestinians. Now it's a question of survival. But I think we have to go beyond survival to the battle of culture and information. And there are people in Israel who are also very anxious to hear what we have to say. We have to provide them with a message that Zionism has never done anything for them. More Israelis are beginning to understand that Israel, despite its enormous military strength and economic and political power, is more insecure than it ever was. There's a reason for that. Since the Israeli leadership is unable to provide them with an understanding of it, we have to do it. So we have a lot of tasks on hand, but they are doable, and they don't involve suicide and a kind of brave but in the end futile throwing of stones and exposing yourself to the depredations of the Israeli military.

What role do you see for the UN in resolving the question of Palestine?

The framework of the UN is absolutely essential. Unfortunately, Arafat and the PLO threw away the UN umbrella when they went into the Madrid talks. They paid lip service to UN Security Council Resolutions 242 and 338. Those resolutions forbid the annexation of territory, the expropriation of further territory, all of which occurred during the Oslo peace process. Now what we as Palestinians have to put pressure on

82 Culture and Resistance

the leadership to do is not to accept any further negotiations with the Israelis unless they accept the principles of 242 and 338. There should be a push on the part of the General Assembly, since the United States has this wretched veto in the Security Council, to make certain that there is protection for Palestinian civilians who are exposed to Israeli gunfire every day of their lives.

You're a lightning rod for criticism, from the National Post *in Canada to the* Wall Street Journal *to* Commentary *to the* New Republic.[9] *How do you respond?*

I don't. It's a total waste of time. These are propagandists who have a racist hatred of Palestinians, Arabs, and Muslims that seems to be irremediable. And besides, it's not the readers of the *New Republic* or the *National Post*. It's their owners. These are wealthy men—Martin Peretz, Conrad Black, Mort Zuckerman, and all the others—who have twisted ideas which they are able to buy people into reading. I suppose it flatters me that they think I'm important enough to keep attacking me. What it does do, in fact, is to interest more people in my work and my writing. That's the way I respond to them, by producing more. I think what they want is my silence. Unless I die, it's not going to happen.

In your 1978 book Orientalism *you wrote, "The life of an Arab Palestinian in the West, particularly in America, is disheartening."[10] Does that situation still obtain today?*

What They Want Is My Silence

What's disheartening is the fact that many of the same prejudices I was attacking, the misrepresentations, the racist assumptions about Arabs and Muslims, are still there. Obviously, I wasn't vain enough to think that my book would turn the tide. But it's enforced every day by the media, which—whether constitutively or out of ignorance or laziness—perpetuates these images, even by people who set out to do different. I'll give you a perfect example. John Burns, who for many years was the *Times* correspondent in the Indian subcontinent, came to see me about five years ago and said that he had planned to take a year's sabbatical with the permission of the editor of the *Times,* Joseph Lelyveld, in order to retool himself as somebody who was interested in Islam and the Arabs. He got a year off. He spent it in Oxford and Cambridge. I saw him once when I was lecturing at Oxford. He was reading up on the Arabs and Islam in order, he said, to be able to cover those things from a different point of view. Not the violence and terrorism, but the diversity of culture, the currents in those societies that went beyond terrorism and violence. He came back after a year and what was the result? Reporting on terrorism and violence among the Arabs and in the Islamic world. So it's built into the media that this is what is permissible. In many ways it's much worse than it was before.

But on the other hand there is a rising tide which is quite evident wherever you go that this is now being combated. There is an alternative media, which you represent, which is quite widespread. There is an enormous amount of informa-

84   Culture and Resistance

tion available on the Internet, and alternative press from various countries, such as England, France, and Israel. So at least from that point of view, my books can be seen in a wider context, which is more encouraging.

There is a decided pressure which I have had directed against me to discourage me from talking and to discourage others from listening to me. They use very punitive means. They threaten. They get people to cancel lectures. It hasn't happened very often, but that's what they try to do. They don't engage you directly. It's very cowardly. Conrad Black, for example, has instructed his writers in England never to say a favorable word about the Palestinians and always to restrain themselves in criticism against Israel. He has failed. According to the brouhaha that he started, many writers, like Ian Gilmour and others, responded, and he wasn't able to keep them down.[11] The situation isn't quite that favorable in this country, because Peretz will not allow a single word of criticism against Israel in the *New Republic*. The *New York Times* hasn't permitted any divergence of views about Palestine on the op-ed pages except a handful of times since the beginning of the Intifada. The rest are all William Safire and Thomas Friedman and the like. So one has to look elsewhere, and there it's not so disheartening.

Noam Chomsky says you're "in an ambivalent position in relation to the media and mainstream culture," because your contributions in terms of literary criticism are recognized and honored. Yet you're "the target of constant vilification."[12]

What They Want Is My Silence

It's very similar to him. He's a well-known, great linguist. He's been celebrated and honored for that. But he's also vilified as an anti-Semite and a Hitler worshiper. The range of stuff has become so crazy, whether against him or me, that it's become kind of funny in a way. But they are insensate. Look at what happened to me with this pebble I threw in South Lebanon.[13] That was covered over the twenty-two-year-old occupation of South Lebanon by the Israelis, the killing of some 17,000 people during the invasion of Lebanon in 1982, the torture of 8,000 people in Khiam prison, only a mile away from where I threw that stone. After a while people begin to ask, Are these people crazy? They are so loony. They're like characters out of Molière, full of "the humors," as they used to be called in the seventeenth century, choleric, unreasonable, stamping their little feet in rage. It's backfiring in many ways. It hasn't stopped Noam, and it hasn't stopped me.

The reverberations of the stone-throwing incident continue. You had been invited by the Freud Society of Vienna to give a talk on May 6. Your invitation was withdrawn.[14]

That was a clear case of pressure. I was invited by the Freud Society in the summer of 2000, well after this incident of the stone, which was published the day after in *Ha'aretz* and then in the American media a couple of days later. That was early July. My invitation was around the middle of August. I accepted on September 1. I gave them the title of the lecture. It wasn't until the middle of February that I got this unannounced letter saying that the lecture was being can-

86 Culture and Resistance

celed. Why? Because, the gentlemen said, "of the political situation in the Middle East and its consequences." I immediately sent him back a letter saying, I would like to know what the connection is between a lecture on Freud in Vienna and the "political situation in the Middle East and its consequences." To this day I haven't received an answer. But the lecture was canceled.

I subsequently found out that what had happened was that they had received funding for an exhibition of Freud's papers in Tel Aviv and were told that if they wanted to exhibit these papers and wanted the funding for it, this was from funders in Israel and America, they would have to cancel my lecture. Dutifully, they did. There was a lot of protest. A dozen of the most distinguished psychoanalysts in the world signed a letter in protest of the Freud Society which was published in the *London Review of Books*.[15] The press in Austria was uniformly hostile. This poor fall guy for them, who was a sociologist who is the head of the board of the Freud Society in Vienna, was forced to say stupid things like, We have to take into account the sensibilities of the Austrian Jewish community, the emergence of Jörg Haider, and memories of the Holocaust, without ever showing any connection between all that and me and my lecture. I think I had the last word when I said, Freud was hounded out of Vienna in the late 1930s by the Nazis, and as a Palestinian I wasn't allowed to speak in Vienna by the same mentality, basically, just a generation or two later.[16]

The upshot of it was that the Freud Museum Institute in London issued an invitation immediately for me to give the same lecture that I was to have given in Vienna on a date of my choosing. I couldn't do it on May 6, Freud's birthday, because of other commitments, but I'm going to do it in December. Four other institutions in Vienna, including the University, the Institute of Human Sciences, and the Middle East Institute, have issued invitations to me to speak in Vienna, which I am going to do in November, despite the Freud Museum's puerile and quite stupid capitulating to outside pressure.

Robert Fisk, Middle East correspondent for The Independent, *comments that "the degree of abuse and outright threats now being directed at anyone—academic, analyst, reporter—who dares to criticise Israel is fast reaching McCarthyite proportions.... Ignorance of the Middle East is now so firmly adhered to in the US that only a few tiny newspapers report anything other than Israel's point of view."[17]*

I did a homemade survey of the major papers in the metropolitan centers, including Los Angeles, New York, Chicago, Atlanta, Boston. They are uniformly reporting from Israel, that is to say, reporters who are stationed in Jerusalem, which is Israel because it's been annexed, or Tel Aviv, and they have very few reporters in the Arab world reporting the Palestinian point of view. Second, they report things that are sent back to their editorial offices in their home bases, and the stories are changed to reflect the same bias, the same line. The mantra is Palestinian violence and Israeli insecurity. That is the theme of all the reporting of incidents in which hundreds of Palestinians have been killed, thousands maimed

88　　　　　　　　**Culture and Resistance**

and wounded, ignoring the reports of Amnesty, Human Rights Watch, the UN committees, and the UN High Commissioner for Refugees' report.

I could give you a dozen citations that are easily verifiable for what is taking place. None of it gets reflected in the major newspapers, and certainly not on the TV screen. Even the so-called virtuous ones, like the *NewsHour* on PBS and National Public Radio, hew to the same line, largely because, and they told me this when I inquired, of letter-writing campaigns or e-mail campaigns that flood the papers or the broadcast headquarters with complaints, obviously orchestrated by Zionist committees, public relations outfits, whatever they are, designed to keep the news focused on Israel and Israel's plight. There are a few intrepid people writing in the *Orlando Sentinel*, the *Seattle Post-Intelligencer*, *Z Magazine*, the *Des Moines Register*, the *Hartford Courant*; you find them here and there, but they are few and far between and do not reach the major newspaper or magazine reading public.

Terrorism is an ongoing focus for the U.S. media. The State Department has just issued its annual report. With the litany of terrorist states, Afghanistan, Pakistan, Iran, Iraq, Libya, Sudan, and Syria, all of them are Muslim majority countries. "Terrorism is a persistent disease," Colin Powell said as he released the report.[18] What geopolitical function does the focus on terrorism serve?

First of all, this relentless pursuit of terrorism is in my opinion almost a kind of criminal thing. It allows the United States to do what it wishes anywhere in the world. Take, for

What They Want Is My Silence   89

example, the 1998 bombing of Sudan. That was done because Bill Clinton was having trouble with Monica Lewinsky. There was a paper-thin excuse that they were bombing a terrorist factory, which turned out to be a pharmaceutical factory producing half the pharmaceutical supply for the country, which was a few weeks later in the grip of a plague.[19] Hundreds of people died as a result of the plague because there were no pharmaceuticals to treat them because of the willful bombing by the United States.

Terrorism has become a sort of screen created since the end of the Cold War by policymakers in Washington, as well as a whole group of people like Samuel Huntington and Steven Emerson, who have their meal ticket in that pursuit. It is fabricated to keep the population afraid, insecure, and to justify what the United States wishes to do globally. Any threat to its interests, whether it's oil in the Middle East or its geostrategic interests elsewhere, is all labeled terrorism, which is exactly what the Israelis have been doing since the mid-1970s so far as Palestinian resistance to their policies are concerned. It's very interesting that the whole history of terrorism has a pedigree in the policies of imperialists. The French used the word terrorism for everything that the Algerians did to resist the French occupation, which began in 1830 and didn't end until 1962. The British used it in Burma, in Malaysia, the same idea. Terrorism is anything that stands in the face of what "we" want to do.

Since the United States is the global superpower, has or pretends to have interests everywhere, from China to Europe to southern Africa to Latin America and all of North America, terrorism becomes a handy instrument to perpetuate this hegemony. Terrorism is now viewed as resistance to globalization. That connection has to be made. I notice, by the way, that Arundhati Roy made that connection as well, that people's movements of resistance against deprivation, against unemployment, against the loss of natural resources, all of that is termed terrorism.[20]

Into this vicious cycle feed a few groups like the bin Laden group and the people he commands, whether they are in Saudi Arabia or Yemen or anywhere else. They're magnified and blown up to insensate proportions that have nothing to do with their real power and the real threat they represent. This focus obscures the enormous damage done by the United States, whether militarily or environmentally or economically, on a world scale that far dwarfs anything that terrorism might do.

Lastly, very little is said about homegrown terrorism, the militias, the armed groups in this country, the Timothy McVeighs. I remember very clearly after the blowing up of the federal building in Oklahoma City, my office was deluged with phone calls because—I think it was Steven Emerson, who was instantly called an expert on terrorism, who said it first—this has all the marks of Middle Eastern terrorism.[21] Immediately they called my office. I happened to be in Canada at the time. About thirty people from the media called. They assumed that because I was from the Middle East I knew something about terrorism and therefore I had some

What They Want Is My Silence 91

insight into the Oklahoma bombing. That cycle of connections is deeply damaging to individuals of Arab and Muslim origin in this country, with the result that during the 2000 election campaign, anything having to do with Islam or the Muslims was used as a way to discredit the others. Hillary Clinton returned a $50,000 contribution from the Muslim Alliance, which is a very conventional, quite politically neutral group, because they smacked of terrorism, she said.[22] Those kinds of labels can be like racial profiling that involves not only African Americans and Latinos but also Muslim Americans.

The U.S. and U.K.-led sanctions against Iraq are clearly crumbling. What accounts for that?

They've failed. In the first place, the point of the sanctions was to bring down Saddam Hussein. Saddam got stronger. Second, the Iraqi civilian population has suffered enormous harm, genocidal harm, thanks to the United Kingdom and the United States. Sixty thousand children are dying every year since the sanctions were imposed.[23] And countless unnumbered others are affected genetically through cancer and other genetically transmitted diseases, not to mention the impoverishment of the entire population. Two UN commissioners of the oil-for-food program resigned because of the inhumanity of the sanctions.[24]

Third, Iraq does not exist, contrary to U.S. policymakers' fantasies, in a vacuum. It is, along with Egypt, one of the central Arab countries. Its economy has always historically been tied to that of its neighbors, especially Jordan. What has happened is that the Jordanians have now been supplied by Iraq with oil at 50 percent of its cost, and so Jordan trades with Iraq. There are other kinds of organic connections between Iraq and its neighbors, including some of the Gulf countries. So the sanctions can't possibly continue in the form that they were envisioned.

As a result, we have Colin Powell traveling throughout the Middle East in February, advocating something called "smart sanctions," which struck me as a complete misnomer and again a fantasy to suggest that the United States can in fact cause people to go against their own interests to line up with the United States.[25] That won't happen. The whole thing has been a total, futile, disastrous policy. The irony of it. The power and wealth and distance of the United States is such that most people have no awareness of the damage that has been caused in the name of the United States and worse, the hatred that has been built up against the United States throughout the Middle East and the Islamic world for no purpose other than to guarantee the continued dominance of a tiny minority, whose interests are tied to this ridiculous and inhuman policy.

One of the countries that has broken the sanctions and actually sent flights into Baghdad is Turkey. It is in the situation of being the site of the major U.S. air base that bombs Iraq and also a country that has invaded northern Iraq, a number of times, in pursuit of Kurdish resistance fighters.

What They Want Is My Silence 93

And which is supplied by the United States in pursuit of its war against the Kurds, to an extent that makes what happened to the Albanians in Kosovo look like a Sunday school picnic. Turkey, one mustn't forget, is in very close alliance with Israel. They have joint military maneuvers. There's a military alliance with the United States and with Israel, and yet, because commercial and regional interests override those strategic interests, Turkey is now trading with and getting oil from Iraq, the second-largest oil supplier in the region. It doesn't seem to be entirely unlikely that Iraq will now trade with Pakistan.

Do you think the Israeli military and economic alliance with Turkey is part of a grand strategy to encircle the Arabs?

No, because Egypt is involved. It's not to encircle the Arabs. It's to encircle what are considered to be intransigent states, like Syria and Iraq and Iran. It's not directed against the Arabs, but rather against those states that are seen to be too anti-Israeli or too sympathetic to the Palestinians. But it's a mindless, irrational strategy, because in the final analysis, although the army is the largest employer in Egypt, and of course it is subservient to the will of the rulers, these are deeply unpopular policies and can't possibly last. It's like Syngman Rhee in South Korea, or Nguyen Cao Ky and Nguyen Van Thieu in Vietnam. U.S. policymakers never learn. They repeat the same mistakes at the same human and economic and political costs. They will persist in doing it, because their education and their perspective is the same, handed down from generation to generation.

Nobel Prize–winner and current Israeli Foreign Minister Shimon Peres recently gave an interview to the Turkish press denying the Armenian genocide.[26]

There too Turkish policy and Israeli policy are very similar. They both have an interest in suppressing knowledge and acknowledgment of what the Turkish government did to the Armenians early in the twentieth century. I'll give you an example. In 1983 there was an Israeli government radio program that was about trying to understand what happened to the Armenians.[27] It was forbidden to go out on the air simply because they used the words "holocaust" and "genocide," which in Israel are reserved only for what happened to the Jews. This kind of policy is perpetuated by what Peres did, stupidly, instead of trying to widen the circle of acknowledgment and understanding of what might happen to people, whether to Rwandans or to Armenians or Bosnians or others elsewhere in the world, where these horrible things have occurred and where all human beings have an interest in making sure that they don't happen again. They want to organize memory in such a way that it's focused exclusively on certain groups and not on other groups that suffered these historical calamities.

Norman Finkelstein has a recent book called The Holocaust Industry.[28] *What do you think about his thesis that there's something like a holocaust industry?*

I think in many ways he's right. In this country there is a determined effort to turn the Holocaust into a kind of secular religion, to make it an object of scholarship in a proprietary sense as part of the Jewish experience and exclusively as part of the Jewish experience. It really ought to be looked at as part of a much wider phenomenon, including the holocaust that occurred here in this country to the Native Americans. It ought to include the terrible travail and experiences of the African Americans who were brought over by the millions to suffer slavery and bondage. The Holocaust industry is correctly identified by Finkelstein as having more to do with the assertion of power than it has with the assertion of historical truth. It's an invidious strain that has very little to do with the actual suffering of Holocaust victims themselves, whether in Germany or in Poland, all of which deserve to be studied, but not within the narrow confines that are to be found today in American universities and elsewhere. They should be seen as part of a larger study of human inhumanity.

You've spoken out on many occasions on the right of return. Are Palestinians making any headway on getting recognition for the issue?

More and more people are aware that there is a right of return. I don't mean only necessarily to Palestine. The right of return is Article 2 of the UN Charter, enshrined in the Uni-

96 **Culture and Resistance**

versal Declaration of Human Rights and every international protocol, that people cannot be driven from their homes or even choose to leave their homes and not have the right also to return. That's the larger principle. As for Palestinians, that, too, is a political point that deserves to be made and is slowly being made. It was left out of the Oslo peace process. Palestinians now constitute the largest number of disenfranchised refugees since World War II still in existence and still to be found in refugee camps.

The right of return can also serve to draw attention to the plight of Palestinians in Arab countries, Lebanon, Syria, and others, where they haven't been patriated and been given rights of residence or work or travel. So it's not just Israel, although Israel is the main cause of this, but elsewhere in the Arab world in general where Palestinians are treated invidiously. I like to think that this is part of a bigger phenomenon drawing attention to the rights of immigrants to enter countries if they've been driven from their own. If they're not able for political and physical reasons to return, they should be given rights of residence wherever they are.

It's a worldwide phenomenon that deeply interests me. We live in a period of migration, of forced travel and forced residence, that has literally engulfed the globe. This has resulted, not only in Israel but in the United States and Britain, in a series of very reactionary immigration laws that are motivated by some myth of purity. Countries like Italy, Sweden, Britain, and the United States have claimed a right to ward off these lesser people who come from Africa and Asia mostly.

What They Want Is My Silence

The principle is the same, whether people are not allowed to return to their homes in Palestine or whether people are not allowed to find new homes in countries like Lebanon or the United States or Sweden because they're considered to be strangers and alien. The whole concept of who is a stranger and who is an alien and who is a native has to be rethought to include the fate of people whose ancestors were exterminated and people who came in and forcibly became settler colonists in countries like Israel and the United States. It's a vast phenomenon and urgently in need of rethinking in ways that I hope the Palestinian right of return movement can dramatize.

You've been teaching for thirty-plus years now. What do you try to impart to your students? How do you instill in them a sense of critical thinking?

It's difficult. We live in an age of packaged and commodified information, the model of which is the media, and I must say even the Internet. You can bring up printed items that have the air of a certain kind of authority and finality which it seems to me the critical mind is obligated to question. First of all, there is for me the duty of the teacher to give information and knowledge, to expose students to things they didn't know about before. I teach mainly literature and philosophy. There are vast numbers of books and authors that deserve to be known that I try to urge people to read. I also try to train people how to read.

Second, I teach people how to read critically, which is to be able not only to see a book for what it is, simply as a book,

98 Culture and Resistance

but to locate it in its context, to understand how it came about, that nothing just happens. It's an act of choice, a series of choices, processes, in which authors and societies are involved. Third, I try to show how these books are parts of, you might say, networks of understanding, information, and knowledge which the students must also take on and challenge, assimilate, and also sift critically to understand how, say, a novel in English might be related to a novel in French or to a novel in English written by a non-English person in Africa, the Caribbean, or America. The point that I want my students to reach is that knowledge and reading are always unfinished. They are always continuing. They require an endless amount of questioning, discovery, and challenge. If I succeed in nothing else, it's to plant the seed of dissatisfaction and relentless questioning in them that doesn't remove at the same time the taste for pleasure and for learning, which are at the core of what we do.

Is the role of the intellectual by definition oppositional?

I think in this society it must be. I believe very much in the individual consciousness. That is the root of all human work. Human understanding cannot take place on a collective scale unless it first takes place on an individual scale. The individual consciousness in our age is bombarded, if it isn't also stifled, by vast amounts of organized and packaged information. Its main goal is to generate a kind of accepting, unquestioning, collective passivity. Most of the time we are bombarded with images that ask us to submit to them and in the end buy them, whether through news or commodities or travel or whatever.

Everything is packaged and up for sale. This is the meaning of the neoliberal market economy, which globalization has foisted on the world, leaving very little room for individual challenge and questioning, whereas large organizations, whether governments or corporations, pursue policies that are virtually blind in many instances, causing widespread environmental destruction, widespread genetic destruction, and the possibility for powerful groups to pursue profit without responsibility. In such a context, the role of the intellectual is to oppose, and I would have thought it an absolutely, perhaps even a desperately needed role. I don't mean just in a negative and silly way; I'm against that. But rather, by oppositional I mean to be able to sift, to judge, to criticize, to choose so that choice and agency returns to the individual. It is important to be a part of another whole, a community that does not have commodified interests and profitable commercial goals in mind. Those are very difficult goals to achieve. But I think they are achievable.

Notes

1 Melissa Radler, "US Backs Israel at UN, Opposes International Monitors," *Jerusalem Post,* August 21, 2001, p. 1.

2 See chapter 2, note 5 above.

3 Deborah Sontag, "Death and Daily Life Link Arab and Israeli," *New York Times,* May 2, 2001, p. A11.

4   The text of the ad ("The Big Lie Is Still Alive") is available online at http://www.ajc.org/InTheMedia/AdvertisementsDetail.asp?did=201&pid=699.

5   Sam Kiley "Israeli Rabbi Calls on God to Annihilate Arabs," *The Times* (London), April 10, 2001.

6   See, among other reports, Serge Schmemann, "Arafat Remains Defiant Amid Rubble of His Compound," *New York Times,* September 22, 2002, p. 1: 8.

7   Tracy Wilkinson, "Palestinian Towns Wobbling on Last Legs," *Los Angeles Times*, December 30, 2002. See also Sara Roy, "Decline and Disfigurement: The Palestinian Economy After Oslo," in *The New Intifada: Resisting Israel's Apartheid,* ed. Roane Carey (New York: Verso, 2001), and Stephen Farrell, "Dying for Work: Five Pay Price at Gaza," *The Times* (London), December 14, 2002.

8   Associated Press, "Vermont Ice Cream Maker in Middle East Controversy," September 24, 1998.

9   See, for example, the scurrilous article by Justus Reid Weiner, "The False Prophet of Palestine," *Wall Street Journal,* August 26, 1999, p. A18.

10   Edward W. Said, *Orientalism* (New York: Pantheon Books, 1978), p. 27.

11   See Charles Glass, "The First Casualty: A Newspaper Proprietor Should Champion, Not Censor, His Writers," *The Observer,* March 18, 2001, p. 27.

12   Maya Jaggi, "Edward Said: Out of the Shadows," *The Guardian* (London), September 11, 1999, p. 6.

13   See Karen W. Arenson, "Columbia Debates a Professor's 'Gesture,'" *New York Times,* October 19, 2000, p. B3.

14   See Dinitia Smith, "Freud Museum Speaking Ban Sparks Said Fury," *The Observer* (London), March 11, 2001, p. 21.

15   Jessica Benjamin et al., Letter to the Freud Society of Vienna, *London Review of Books* 23: 6 (March 22, 2001). Available online at http://www.lrb.co.uk/v23/n06/letters.html.

16 Smith, "Freud Museum Speaking Ban Sparks Said Fury," p. 21.

17 Robert Fisk, "I Am Being Vilified for Telling the Truth About Palestinians," *The Independent* (London), December 13, 2000, p. 5.

18 Marc Lacey, "Attacks Were Up Last Year, U.S. Terrorism Report Says," *New York Times,* May 1, 2001, p. A14.

19 See James Risen, "To Bomb Sudan Plant, or Not: A Year Later, Debates Rankle," *New York Times,* October 27, 1999, p. A1, and Tim Weiner and Steven Lee Myers, "U.S. Notes Gaps in Data About Drug Plant but Defends Attack," *New York Times,* September 3, 1998, p. A6.

20 Arundhati Roy, Interview with David Barsamian, *The Progressive* 65: 4 (April 2001). See also Arundhati Roy, *Power Politics,* 2nd ed. (Cambridge: South End Press, 2001).

21 See Felicity Barringer, "Terror Experts Use Lenses of Their Specialties," *New York Times,* September 24, 2001, p. C1.

22 Dean E. Murphy, "Mrs. Clinton Says She Will Return Money Raised by a Muslim Group," *New York Times,* October 26, 2000, p. A1.

23 See Anthony Arnove, ed., *Iraq Under Siege: The Deadly Impact of Sanctions and War,* 2nd ed. (Cambridge: South End Press, 2002), p. 79.

24 Arnove, *Iraq Under Siege,* p. 47.

25 John F. Burns, "Iraq Defiant as U.S. Lobbies Arabs on Shift in Sanctions," *New York Times,* February 25, 2001, p. 1: 4.

26 Robert Fisk, "Peres Stands Accused Over Denial of 'Meaningless' Armenian Holocaust," *The Independent* (London), April 18, 2001, p. 13.

27 Edward W. Said, *The Politics of Dispossession: The Struggle for Palestinian Self-Determination, 1969–1994* (New York: Pantheon Books, 1994), p. 253.

28 Norman Finkelstein, *The Holocaust Industry: Reflections on the Exploitation of Jewish Suffering* (New York: Verso, 2000).

Origins of Terrorism

KGNU, Boulder, Colorado, September 24, 2001

The events of September 11, 2001, have bewildered and confused many Americans. What might be a good place to start, to give people some understanding as to the context and background that would motivate terrorist hijackers?

Speaking as a New Yorker, it was a shocking and terrifying event, I mean, particularly the scale of it. It was designed to shock and terrify and paralyze and do a whole lot of terrible and, in my opinion, inexcusable things.

But it was obviously the result of a great deal of planning, as well as very audacious—some might even say brilliant—execution. And, at the bottom of it, an implacable desire to do harm. Not quite indiscriminate, I would say, because it was aimed at symbols: the World Trade Center, the heart of American capitalism, and the Pentagon, the headquarters of the American military establishment. But it was not meant to be argued with. It wasn't part of any negotiation and obvi-

104   **Culture and Resistance**

ously no message was intended with it. It spoke for itself, which is unusual.

I think that it comes out of a long dialectic of U.S. involvement abroad that spans the entire past century. Involvement in the affairs of the Islamic world, the oil-producing world, the Arab world, the Middle East. All those areas of the world that are considered to be essential to U.S. interests and security that include oil and strategic power; the control and positioning of the United States in the Persian Gulf; the protection of allies like Israel, Saudi Arabia, and others. And through this dialectic, and a relentlessly unfolding series of interactions, the United States has played, to the residents of this area, a very distinctive role, which most Americans, I think, have been either shielded from or are simply unaware of.

It's important to understand first of all that there are two worlds here—there's the world of people who live in that environment and the world of people who live in the United States. And there really is very little in common between them. There never has been much direct contact as there had been, for example, between Great Britain and the Islamic world, including Afghanistan, and certainly the Gulf and India and, for example, Iraq. The United States has been protected by its enormous distance from the place, including the Atlantic Ocean, the Mediterranean, and the sheer difficulty of getting there. But there's also been another barrier—and that is, of course, language and religion.

This is an area of the world, starting, let's say, in Bosnia and moving East, all across Central Asia and then down into the

Middle East, Pakistan, Bangladesh, Indonesia to the East and then the Arab countries in the middle, all across north Africa, which is largely Muslim, where 1.2 billion Muslims live, where the United States is seen in two quite different ways. One, the official United States, the United States of armies and interventions, such as in 1953 when it overthrew the nationalist government of Mohammad Mossadegh in Iran and brought back the shah. The United States that has been involved first in the Gulf War and then in the tremendously damaging—damaging to civilians, that is—sanctions, against Iraq. The United States is the supporter of Israel against the Palestinians, first in the establishment of the state in 1948, then in the occupation of 1967, the Lebanese war, the invasion of Lebanon by Israel in 1982, the Intifadas of 1987 and 2000. The United States supplies Israel with enormous amounts of weapons. So if you live in the area, you see these things as part of a continuing drive for dominance and with it, a kind of obduracy to the wishes and desires and aspirations of the people there.

I think that most Arabs and Muslims feel that the United States hasn't really been paying much attention to their desires, but has been pursuing its policies for its own sake, without much in the way of explanation or attempts to somehow justify them. And above all, pursuing these policies not according to many of the principles that the United States proclaims are its own: democracy, self-determination, freedom of speech, freedom of assembly, and its commitment to international law. It's very hard, for example, to justify the thirty-four-year-old occupation of the West Bank and Gaza—140 Israeli settle-

Culture and Resistance

ments and roughly 400,000 settlers brought with the support and financing of the United States—and say this is part of U.S. adherence to international law and UN resolutions.

So all of this is a record that keeps building up in an area in which—and here we come now to the really sad part—the rulers have been supported by the United States against the wishes of the people. And there is a general sense in which the United States is flouting its own principles in order to maintain such governments and regimes in power and really have very little to do with the large number of people who are dominated by these regimes.

The result is a kind of schizophrenic picture of the United States. Every Arab or Muslim that I know is tremendously interested in the United States. Many of them send their children here for education. Many of them come here for vacations. Some do business here or come for training. They are perfectly aware of what an extraordinary country this is on the one hand. And on the other, there's the other view which is that the U.S. government is a different thing and is quite impervious to the appeals of conscience and decency and international law. Now, in this rather heady mixture of violence and, how shall I say it, policies that are remarkably unpopular right down to the last iota, it's not hard for demagogues, especially people who claim to speak in the name of religion, in this case Islam, to raise a crusade against the United States, to raise a banner and say that we must defend against this policy and somehow bring America down; we have to first of all resist and second we have to fight them.

Origins of Terrorism   107

And don't forget, ironically, and this is the last point to be made here, that many of these people, including Osama bin Laden and the Afghan Taliban as well as the mujahideen, the fighters with them, were in fact supported and nourished by the United States in the early 1980s during the Soviet invasion of Afghanistan, when it was thought that to rally Islam against godless communism would be doing the Soviet Union a very bad turn indeed and that in fact transpired. I remember in 1986 a group of mujahideen came to Washington and were greeted by President Reagan, who called them "freedom fighters."[1]

This was the going mantra for a long time. And then there was the sense of betrayal that many ordinary Muslims feel, living, as I say, in poverty and desperation. Above all, I think, in desperation—desperation and ignorance. It's not difficult to start rallying people in the name of Islam. These preachers, by the way, are completely self-appointed spokespeople of Islam. They don't represent Islam in any formal sense. They're not imams, they're not sheiks. They are self-appointed warriors for Islam, and in the case of Osama bin Laden in particular, who is a Saudi, a man who feels himself to be a patriot because U.S. forces are in Saudi Arabia, which is sacred because of the prophet Mohammed, and who feels it is his duty to start fulminating against the United States, and turning against the people who brought them there. There is also this great sense of triumphalism, that just as we defeated the Soviet Union, we can do this. And out of this, this sense of desperation and pathological religion, there develops an

108 **Culture and Resistance**

all-encompassing drive to harm and hurt, without regard for the innocent and the uninvolved, which was the case in New York.

Now to understand all of this is of course not at all to condone it. What terrifies me is that we're entering a phase here where speaking about this, as something that can be understood historically, without any sympathy or condoning of it, is going to be forbidden, and thought of as unpatriotic. It's very dangerous. It is precisely incumbent on every citizen to quite understand the world we're living in and the history, of which we are not only a part, but in many ways forming as a superpower.

In your article in the London Observer *entitled "Islam and the West Are Inadequate Banners," you say the U.S. drive for war "uncannily resembles Captain Ahab in pursuit of Moby Dick."[2] Tell me what you have in mind there.*

Captain Ahab in Melville's great novel *Moby Dick* was a man possessed with an obsessional drive to pursue the white whale which had harmed him, which had torn his leg out, to the ends of the earth, no matter what happened.[3] In the final scene of the novel, Captain Ahab is being borne out to sea, wrapped around the white whale with the rope of his own harpoon and going obviously to his death. It was a scene of almost suicidal finality. I think that in this whipping up of the American people, the government has indulged in a similar drive for retribution, for perfectly understandable reasons— that is to say, this is a tremendous blow inflicted on the United

States. There's no question that a great deal of harm and terrible loss was inflicted on us as a people and as a society. That anything goes—the rising tide of war and retribution and bringing to justice and wanted dead or alive, all the words that George Bush has used in public—suggests not so much an orderly and considered progress towards bringing the man to justice according to international norms, but rather something apocalyptic, something of the order of the criminal atrocity itself.

I feel that that is simply making matters a lot, lot worse, because there are always consequences. And it would seem to me that to give Osama bin Laden, who has been demonized—he has in fact been turned into Moby Dick, made a symbol of all that's evil in the world—to give him a kind of mythological proportion is really playing his game. I think we need to secularize the man, we need to bring him down to the realm of reality, treat him as a criminal, as a man who is a demagogue, who has unlawfully unleashed violence against innocent people, and punish him accordingly. Not to bring down the world around him and ourselves, if necessary. But to deal with him as one deals with people who committed horrible crimes. It's inevitable that Americans feel now that they are at war with Islam. Despite the calls of the president and Mayor Giuliani and others to say we are not at war with Islam, the fact is that everywhere you look in this society there've been dozens, if not hundreds, of incidents against Muslims and people who look like Muslims to the people attacking them.[4]

110 **Culture and Resistance**

There was the case of a Sikh killed in Arizona and others whose properties have been defaced.[5]

A Pakistani was murdered in Texas.[6]

Yes, and many people in New York have felt the brunt of this. People have been visited by the police and the FBI because they have Middle Eastern names and so on. So there's an atmosphere not only of mobilization but of a descending fear, and a kind of paranoia which befits a country at war against a disembodied kind of super enemy called Osama bin Laden and Islam. I really think that the media has played a very important role in all of this by insisting on the same images over and over again, by demonizing, by repeating and not permitting what in effect is reflection. In this desire to report what's happening, the media has simply fallen into the prevailing mood and has rushed it to further judgement and to further action which I think is terribly hasty and in my opinion probably going to produce more problems than it solves.

There seems to be a certain pattern at work here, as you suggest. First, in the 1970s, the demonization of Arafat and the PLO, followed by Ayatollah Khomeini, Muammar Qaddafi, Saddam Hussein, and now Osama bin Laden.

There's certainly that and also, at least in the case of Saddam and Osama bin Laden, there's been an unwillingness to state the complicity of the United States in the rise of these figures to power. Certainly as I mentioned about bin Laden,

Origins of Terrorism 111

but also in case of Saddam, who was nurtured by the United States as an enemy of Iran. He was given a lot of arms and support by the United States in the period preceding his occupation of Kuwait.

But you know, what is quite worrisome in all of this is the absence of attempts at analysis and reflection rather than attempts to differentiate and define. I mean take the word "terrorism." "Terrorism" has become synonymous now with anti-Americanism, which in turn has become synonymous with being critical of the United States, which in turn has become synonymous with being unpatriotic. That's an unacceptable series of equations. And I think what we need is to go back, for example, to the debates in the United Nations during the 1970s as to what terrorism is. I mean you can't say about mujahideen in Afghanistan in 1980 fighting the Soviets that they were "freedom fighters," and then say that now that they are trying to defend against the incursion of other countries into Afghanistan they are terrorists. Particularly in that there seems to be an undeclared or semi-declared war against the Taliban, who you know are not an attractive bunch by any means. I think the definition of terror and terrorism has to be more precise, so that we are able, since we have this great power as a nation, to discriminate between, for example, what it is that the Palestinians are doing to fight the Israeli military occupation, which has been there for almost thirty-five years now and terrorism of the sort that resulted in the World Trade Center bombing. Besides, there is also state terrorism.

112　　　　　　　**Culture and Resistance**

Eqbal Ahmad of Pakistan, a noted scholar and activist once told me that terrorism is the poor man's B-52.[7]

On one level I think that's certainly true, that is to say, the weapons of the weak are likely to be this kind, speaking now not of course on the level of what took place at the World Trade Center. I'd like to make a distinction between that and the kind of terror that involves, for example, a young man from Gaza living in the most horrendous conditions—of overpopulation, poverty, ignorance, hunger, most of it, in fact I would say 90 percent of it, imposed by Israel as part of its occupation and its siege policies against Palestinians—strapping dynamite around himself and then throwing himself into a crowd of Israelis. I've never condoned or agreed with it, but at least it is understandable as a result of a desperate human being who feels himself being crowded out of life and all of his surroundings, his fellow citizens, other Palestinians, his parents, sisters, and brothers, all of them dying or being hurt, wanting to do something, to strike back. That can be understood as the act of a desperate person trying to free herself or himself from what he thinks are unjustly imposed conditions. It's not something I agree with but at least you could understand it.

Now, here we're talking about something different, because these people are obviously not desperate and poor refugee camp dwellers. The people who perpetrated the terror of the World Trade Center and Pentagon attacks were obviously middle-class, educated enough to be able to go to flight

Origins of Terrorism 113

school in Florida, and could speak English. This is now transcending the political and moving into the metaphysical. And it's a leap that I think is very important to keep one's eye on, because it suggests the kind of cosmic quality—and, I would also say, the demagogical quality—of the minds at work here. They refuse to engage in or have no interest in dialogue or political organization or persuasion of the sort that makes political change and improves one's situation versus this kind of thing which is bloody-minded destruction for no other reason than to do it. Note that there was no claim for this terror bombing. There was no political message behind it. There were no demands. There were no statements. It was a silent piece of terror imposed on a population without discrimination or negotiation. I can't say that this is the poor person's B-52 bombing.

But I would also want to add that some of the things that powers like Britain, the United States, and France have done against lesser people, like bombing them from the air, where the bomber cannot be reached by essentially defenseless people, are also inexcusable. This is what the Israelis are doing in the West Bank and Gaza, using F-16s to attack Palestinian homes, which are completely undefended—there is no Palestinian army, or air force, or anti-aircraft capability—I think that too has the structure of terror. It's meant to impose fear, it's indiscriminate, and there is no chance for any response. It is pure destruction for the sake of destruction and terrorizing people. So, we're in an area where a lot of unpleasant things

114   **Culture and Resistance**

done by them and done by us, whoever them and us are, resemble each other rather too closely.

Again, Eqbal Ahmad commented that "revolutionary terror if ever engaged in must be sociologically and psychologically selective." He said, "Don't hijack a plane.... Don't kill children." And then he points out that "the great revolutions, the Chinese, the Vietnamese, the Algerian, and the Cuban, never engaged in hijacking type of terrorism."[8]

They didn't and it's important to remember that they were somewhat earlier than the period of the great hijackings of the late 1960s and early 1970s, when jet travel had become more prevalent and much more symbolic of national communication across borders.

But did you see any revolutionary component to these actions?

No, of course not. That's what I was saying earlier. There was no message in it, no attempt to change people's minds. It's not part of anything. The Algerians, in fact, did use terror. They put bombs in restaurants and cafes in Algiers, killing French people. It's not something I myself approve of or would advocate in any way, but it was part of a political movement to rid Algeria of the French occupation, which had been there for 130 years. The September 11 attack is part of nothing. It's a vague, and unstated, and unclear mass attack, involving exclusively innocent people as its victims and with no conceivable end in sight except terror for its own sake. In that respect, it's a kind of metaphysical leap into another realm—the realm of crazy abstraction and mythologi-

Origins of Terrorism   **115**

cal generalities, involving people who in my opinion have hijacked Islam for purposes of their own. It's very important not to fall into that trap and try to respond by a metaphysical retaliation of some sort.

Parts of the media and political commentary seem to be echoing Kurtz in The Heart of Darkness *when he said, "Exterminate all the brutes."[9] Robert Kaplan, an* Atlantic Monthly *writer and author of* The Coming Anarchy, *said on NPR that there "is a kind of existential hatred of ... the West."[10] Dan Rather, the CBS news anchor, said of the terrorists on* Late Night with David Letterman, *"They see themselves as the world's losers." They are "crazy people. They are haters."[11] And then he began to cry.*

It's hard for me to explain Dan Rather and Robert Kaplan, neither of whom I particularly admire or look to for insight. But there is no question that in the case of people like Osama bin Laden and others who speak that language, I don't think they think of themselves as losers at all. I think they think of themselves as the bearers of a mighty message. These are people appointed, obviously by themselves, who feel within themselves the enthusiasm and the confidence of a people bearing in a kind of twisted way the burden of a great civilization responding to the attacks of the barbarians.

I think it's wrong, very wrong, to use words like winners and losers. To them, the West represents materialism, a kind of vulgarity, the ubiquitous videos and pornographic films. A monolithic creation that they've made, just as most people tend to make of Islam, a kind of unitary, monolithic thing. It

116   **Culture and Resistance**

works in both directions; to them, the West represents everything that's ugly and a blight on the world. Therefore it's their role to purify and do God's work. This is a rhetoric that works for whoever uses it, whether on one side or the other, assuming that there are really two sides. Obviously there are many more, but the people who think of themselves as us versus them using that binary opposition, whether Americans or others, have lost touch with precisely the kind of reality which human beings ought to be protecting, namely its variety, its diversity, its concreteness, and not these ridiculous—to me—mythological and religious abstractions, or pseudo-religious abstractions, in which everybody feels that he or she is an instrument of God. I don't think it's a matter of losers or winners—it's a matter of winners all around in this instance.

There seems to be a little more nuanced coverage and analysis, at least in Europe, as to what is going on. For example, Matthew Parris, a former Conservative Party member of the British Parliament wrote in *The Times* of London "Do they not know that when you kill one bin Laden you sow twenty more. Playing the world's policeman is not the answer to the catastrophe in New York."[12] And then Dario Fo, the Italian playwright who won the Nobel Prize for Literature in 1997 said that "The great speculators wallow in an economy that every year kills tens of millions of people with poverty.... Regardless of who carried out the massacre," referring to the events in New York and Washington, D.C., "this

Origins of Terrorism

violence is the legitimate daughter of the culture of violence, hunger, and inhumane exploitation."[13]

In general, the view outside the United States necessarily is more nuanced and different because these countries have not been hit. That's one major thing to note. The other thing is that these are smaller post-imperial countries; Britain no longer has an empire to defend; whatever sense of mission and importance it feels, it derives from its association with the United States. That's the meaning of Blair coming along and saying that we are shoulder to shoulder and so on. He's trying to, as it were, bask in the light of the American super-power. But there's also another thing. There is in general, around the world, a sense that partly because of size, different countries are closer to each other, Europeans and Middle Easterners are closer to each other in distance and in history. There's a sense in which we're all involved in the same element, which I think one has to call reality or history, and feel the need to be more analytical, to be more considerate, to be more reflective.

I suppose also there's a certain amount of resentment and jealousy of the United States for its enormous power, which Europeans have felt as something at times oppressive. So, it's a mix of things that allows in the media different views and different interpretations. I found it, in the beginning, in the first few days after the disaster of September 11, depressingly monochromatic in the United States. There's been essentially the same analysis over and over again, and very little attention

118   **Culture and Resistance**

paid to different views or allowances made for different views and interpretations and reflections. Because I think we have a tendency in this country to regard historical analysis as a form of condoning what happened. It's not that at all. You can try to understand what's happening without in the least condoning what is in fact a terrorist crime. But there is also a considered anxiety about the consequences of too hasty an action, which the country is obviously embarked on. There's an anxiety about that; people speak out who want to vary the tone somewhat so that people draw back a bit. And I think it's been noticeable in some of the remarks of even the government. There is a noticeable difference in the language used by Donald Rumsfeld and Paul Wolfowitz at the defense department and say someone like Powell, who's altogether more cautious. He's bureaucratic, it's true, but I think he is aware of the different sensibilities that make up the world we live in.

Do you get the feeling that it's 1990 again? There's a Bush in the White House and a coalition is being formed to take military action against, in this case one of the poorest countries in the world, a country— Afghanistan—that the CIA says does not even have a functioning government.

No, I don't feel it quite so much, except in the atmosphere here, but I think more and more people are beginning to draw back a little bit; there isn't quite the rush you had in 1990, because there isn't, really, a material embodied front or frontier. What we're talking about is a vague thing called terrorism, which as I said has yet to be defined. You can't limit

Origins of Terrorism

terrorism to Osama bin Laden. There are many other kinds of terrorism, obviously, that ought to be herded under that particular rubric. There isn't a particular place—except for Afghanistan, which is hardly, as you've just said, the kind of formidable challenge represented in 1990 by Iraq with its huge army and air force and missiles. And there doesn't seem to be a goal. To say that we're going to end countries or exterminate terrorism or eradicate it, and that it's a long war over many years, with many different instruments, and so on, suggests a much more open-ended and much more complex and drawn out conflict for which, I think, most Americans aren't prepared.

So there is a bit of déjà vu here but there's also an added ingredient—which is the uncertain or the indefinable, the proportions of this war, which may include up to sixty countries that supposedly harbor terrorists. How the United States is going to face what is in fact a super complex phenomenon with a very strong mix of planes and soldiers and navies, and so on, is yet to be determined. There isn't a clear goal in sight. And as Matthew Parris mentioned, even if you find Osama bin Laden, it's quite clear that his organization has spun out from him and is now independent of him. And there will be others who will appear and reappear. This is why I think we need a much more precise, much more defined, much more patiently constructed campaign, as well as one that surveys not just the terrorists' presence but the root causes of it, which are ascertainable, and one can find them.

120   **Culture and Resistance**

In Queens, not far from where you're sitting on the Upper West Side of Manhattan, lives a man named Emmanuel Constant of Haiti. He is accused of war crimes in Haiti, human rights violations, and he's been indicted. Haiti has been trying get him out of the United States and back to Haiti.[14] What might happen if the Haitian air force or navy started attacking the United States for harboring a war criminal?

Exactly. I think the question contains its own answer. It's virtually unthinkable, and only the United States, in its tremendous power and global reach can even contemplate doing things such as what seems to be planned. I mean, I don't have any more information than anyone else, but it does seem to be a major transnational campaign, I would say transcontinental campaign, full of interventions in the affairs of countries who are going to be tried and obviously found wanting for their terrorist crimes.

The idea that there is a kind of secret tribunal sitting in Washington deciding which countries should be hit, and that there's a debate within the intelligence community as to which countries deserve bombing, is unacceptable. No individual, state, or government should be in the possession of such a desire and of such a capacity to execute that desire.

The just response to this terrible event in New York—again, I speak as a New Yorker who feels very aggrieved by the horrible attack on this city in which all of us have lost friends and suffered from the consequences—this should be not taken under the wings of the Unites States exclusively but sent immediately to the world community, the

Origins of Terrorism 121

international community, the United Nations. The rule of international law should be marshaled for this as well as for other events, but it's probably too late because the United States has never done that, it's always gone it alone, as it did in Iraq, summoning the UN at the very end after the course of action had been determined.

Why did the United States make efforts, at least, to bring, with its allies, accused war criminals before a specially constructed UN war crimes tribunal for the former Yugoslavia at the Hague?

That's a very good question. But first of all this is a different government. Since he came into office, George Bush has made it absolutely clear that unilateralism is the key word of this administration, and that it wants to do things as it wishes for interests defined exclusively by the United States. There's been a trend towards unilateralism in U.S. foreign policy for a long time and I think it is being accentuated now, and perhaps understandably so because of the single-minded focus on the United States in this attack. Inconsistency and peculiar behavior of this sort is one of the cornerstones of U.S. foreign policy.

In your introduction to the updated version of Covering Islam: How the Media and the Experts Determine How We See the Rest of the World, *you say that "Malicious generalizations about Islam have become the last acceptable form of denigration of foreign culture in the West."[15] Talk about the role of popular culture in shaping views on Arabs, Muslims, and Islam. Jack Shaheen has a new book out, called*

122   **Culture and Resistance**

Reel Bad Arabs, *about how Hollywood has vilified Arabs, Muslims, and Islam.*[16] *Do you think that's an important area to examine?*

Very much so. I've thought so from the beginning, and I started to write about this subject in my book *Orientalism*. There is an age-old structure of Islam and I suppose the Arabs along with it—by the way, many people think Afghanistan is part of the Arab world—where discriminations are not made, and where it's assumed that we're talking about a quintessential core of attributes, most of them fantasies about the Other with a capital O. So that the Muslim is thought of as being what we are not: fanatical, violent, lustful, irrational, and so on. That idea has persisted because it's based very deeply in religious roots where Islam is thought of as a kind of competitor of Christianity. Islam arises out of the same soil as Christianity, the religion of Abraham, first in Judaism, then Christianity, then in Islam. There was also a long period of approximately 800 years, where Islam dominated Europe, when the Muslim conquests, the Arab conquests, begin in the middle of the seventh century and continue until the fifteenth century.

That sense of Islam as a threatening Other has continued. Plus, of course, the polemical quality of the knowledge about Islam and the Arabs that develops during the colonial period in what I called orientalism, where the study of the Other has a lot to do with the control and dominance of Europe and the West generally in the Islamic world. I must say that very little has changed. If you look at the curricula of most universities

Origins of Terrorism

and schools in this country, considering our long encounter with the Islamic world, there is very little there that you can get hold of that is really informative about Islam. And if you look at the popular media you'll see that the stereotype that begins with Rudolph Valentino in *The Sheik* has really remained and developed into the transnational villain of television and film and popular culture in general.[17]

It is very easy to make wild generalizations about Islam. All you have to do is read almost any issue of the *New Republic* and you'll see Islam associated with radical evil, and the idea that the Arabs have a depraved culture, and so forth. These are impossible generalizations to make virtually about any other religion or ethnic group in the world today in the United States, where there is a great sensitivity, as there should be, to African Americans, Asian Americans, Latin Americans, and so on. But here this thing persists, and one of the main reasons for its persistence has been the absence of a real engagement on the part of Muslims and Arabs in this debate.

The reasons for that are complicated, too long to examine here, but there has been remarkable unawareness in the Islamic and Arab world of what the West and residents of Western countries—now one shouldn't generalize—for the most part see as the Muslim or the Arab. There isn't a cultural policy, there isn't a sense of engaging in a debate or dialogue. A dialogue of cultures is absent so far as Islam is concerned, so far as the Arabs are concerned. Israel plays a great role in all of this. People feel that if you, and I've had this in my own experience, try to talk about the Arab world, if you try to

124　　　　**Culture and Resistance**

bring an Arab writer to America, there's always an outcry as to why isn't there balance? Why didn't you bring an Israeli writer? Or in some ways, if you talk about Arab culture and Arab civilization, you are somehow being anti-Israel. That's a very constant structure with which one has to deal. The ground is not easy to negotiate because it is full of political traps and pitfalls.

I want to add something about the role of higher education. If you look at Columbia University, which has a Middle East languages department, which has a religion department, we don't regularly offer a course on the Koran. Studying the Koran is necessary to an understanding of Islam. It's as simple as that. It's like studying Christianity without looking at the Bible, without looking at the New Testament. It's like studying Judaism without looking at the Old Testament. This is, alas, the case of studying Islam, where you look at summaries in books and accounts by Western scholars of what Islam is rather than looking at the main text itself which, in Islam, plays a much greater role than either the gospels in Christianity or the Torah in Judaism.

Returning to Covering Islam, *in your introduction you say that "A core of 'experts' on the Islamic world has grown to prominence, and during a crisis they are brought out to pontificate on formulaic ideas about Islam on news programs or talk shows."[18] A prestigious talk program on PBS is the nightly one hour* Charlie Rose Show. *I have the guest list from the first week after the September 11th attacks. Let me read you some of the names: Wesley Clark, Sandy Berger, Anthony Lewis,*

Frank Rich, David Halberstam, Jim Hoagland, Mort Zuckerman, and three times Fouad Ajami, who is a regular CBS pundit who moves seamlessly onto PBS.

It shows you the emphasis, which is to treat things such as this, which is, in effect, a terrible event not just in the United States but one having vast international consequences, ramifications, and roots, as essentially a matter of security and military strategy. Not every one of these guests that you mentioned is in the same boat, but I would say that the emphasis is largely on those sorts of things and none of them with the exception of Ajami can be considered somebody who knows anything at all, even in an educated way, about the Islamic or Arab worlds. None of them. Ajami is an expert who has made it quite plain that he has cast his lot with the American right-wing, the neo-conservative movement. He takes very conciliatory positions vis-à-vis Israel, and because he is an Arab and a Muslim, he is seen as an ideal informant for talk shows. Whereas in fact, on the basis of what he has published and the things that he has said, he has revealed himself to be a man of no particular intellectual interest, who nobody that I know of in the field and in the Islamic and Arab world even knows, much less takes seriously. It's a remarkable case of cognitive dissonance. Experts are treated as such without either the competence or the stature, or the work and the knowledge that such a deference implies. It's really quite striking. Whereas I can think quite easily of half a dozen people in this country who would do a much

126   **Culture and Resistance**

better and much more informed job on matters having to do with the Islamic and Arab world than Ajami.

Talk about two wings of the Islamic world that are going to be affected by military action—Egypt in the West and Pakistan in the East.

These are very large issues to consider but the Egyptian government has been beset by Islamic movements that began basically as a part of the nationalist community in Egypt, say in the 1930s with the rise of the Muslim Brotherhood, which was anti-British, anti-imperialist, anti-monarchical. Of course, always with the aim of establishing an Islamic state in what is predominantly an Islamic country, although Egypt isn't entirely Islamic. There is an important minority of Coptic Christians who feel themselves to be just as Egyptian as the Muslim Egyptians. In any case, that community of Muslim nationalists has shifted to one that has become highly, in my terms anyway, reactionary, that sees itself as bearing the burden of originary, primitive Islam, to try to return Egypt to the Sharia, to try to return Egypt to seventh century Mecca, to destroy the intrusions of modern civilization. They, of course, have grabbed public attention because they're armed, they're relatively well-organized, and some of their offshoots are capable of suicide missions of the sort that would involve the killing of tourists and the assassination of Anwar Sadat. They are a disruptive and insurrectionary force.

This doesn't mean that all the pious people, the women who wear hejabs and the men who wear the robes and grow beards, are all part of this. There is also a large protest group

Origins of Terrorism

inside Egypt that has split against the government in its policies, mainly economic and foreign policies that have created a class of impoverished university graduates who appear by the hundreds of thousands every year with no jobs, no opportunities, no easy place to live, no way to earn a living and take care of a family. Islam groups them all together.

The government has played a very dangerous game with them. It has sometimes submitted to their demands, for example, to censor and ban books that are considered pornographic and anti-Islamic; to file cases against professors and writers and public personalities; to go after communities thought of as deviant, whether gay or religious. Every so often the government leans over and throws them a sop and bans programs on television and bans novels and so on rather than taking a line that is quite clear because they find it difficult to do this.

In Pakistan, on the other hand, there is a tradition of Islamic insurrection which has been quite unsuccessful. Whenever there has been an opportunity for elections to determine whether an Islamic government is wanted or not, they inevitably lose. But they, too, are capable of disruptions, assassinations, and so on. They also express the dissatisfactions with what is a skewed economy. This is a nuclear power that can't resolve problems of poverty and famine and unemployment in the large cities like Karachi. We're dealing with very unstable mixes here. Now, to have imposed upon them the burden of a massive military action of the United States can unsettle them profoundly. In places like Pakistan, the idea of this military

128   **Culture and Resistance**

government of Pervez Musharraf being destabilized by an Islamic or a pro-Taliban movement is more threatening because of the nuclear capability, which any government that comes to power will have. It's not a pleasant thing to contemplate.

A front-page photograph in the September 22nd New York Times shows two Pakistani policemen beating and kicking an unarmed demonstrator. Four Pakistanis were killed in Karachi.[19]

Of course, it is a military government and the idea is that we're mobilizing and we are going to do this with the United States. Obviously there are economic rewards, some of their debt is going to be forgiven.[20] There's going to be more economic aid and the stature of Pervez Musharraf's government will be enhanced by the United States. But as with all of these interventions, the results are going to be, in the long run, more negative than they're going to be positive.

But the situation is rich with ironies, particularly in Pakistan, which nurtured the mujahideen during the 1980s and actually created the Taliban and helped install them into power.

Yes, and still does. The Pakistani intelligence services are really—how should I put it—the controllers of the Taliban. There's a healthy back and forth in trade and support, and drug trafficking between Afghanistan and Pakistan that is quasi-official. It's not just one or two people. It involves whole branches of the Pakistani secret services. That's not so easily controlled once the violence begins.

Origins of Terrorism 129

Finally, what are some good sources of information?

There's a whole series of writings about Afghanistan. I would start with the works of the man you mentioned, Eqbal Ahmad, who died two years ago, a dear friend.[21] I would say he is the one essential figure that we ought to have with us because he knew Afghanistan. He himself was Pakistani. He knew the West. He knew the Arab world. He was a Muslim. He was a man of modern sensibility and vast historical information. I'd begin with the writings of Eqbal Ahmad. A whole series of essays, interviews with you, are available. I would say that on questions having to do with Arabs or Islam, there's a whole library of material. Certainly the works of Albert Hourani and Philip Hitti.[22] On contemporary Egypt, there's a vast library, as there is on Pakistan and Afghanistan. I think what we ought to try to get at are authoritative sources that are not polemical and are not Defense Department manuals for conquest and war.

Notes

1   Eqbal Ahmad, *Confronting Empire*, p. 134. See also Eqbal Ahmad, *Terrorism: Theirs and Ours* (New York: Seven Stories Press/Open Media, 2001), p. 4.

2   Edward W. Said, "Islam and the West Are Inadequate Banners," *The Observer* (London), September 16, 2001, p. 27.

3   Herman Melville, *Moby Dick, or the Whale* (New York: Modern Library, 1992).

4   Darryl Fears, "Hate Crimes Against Arabs Surge, FBI Finds," *Washington Post*, November 26, 2002, p. A2.

130 Culture and Resistance

5 See Phuong Ly and Petula Dvora, "Japanese Americans Recall '40s Bias, Understand Arab Counterparts' Fear," *Washington Post,* September 20, 2001, p. B1.

6 Somini Sengupta, "Torn Between Silence and Open Discussion," *New York Times,* September 19, 2001, p. B10.

7 Eqbal Ahmad, personal conversation with the author.

8 Eqbal Ahmad, "Terrorism: Theirs and Ours," presentation at the University of Colorado, Boulder, October 12, 1998. Transcript available from Alternative Radio.

9 Joseph Conrad, *The Heart of Darkness* (New York: Penguin Books, 1999), p. 87.

10 Liane Hansen, Interview with Robert Kaplan, *Weekend Edition Sunday,* National Public Radio (NPR), September 23, 2001.

11 David Letterman, Interview with Dan Rather, *Late Night with David Letterman,* September 18, 2001.

12 Matthew Parris, "The Bigger They Come the Harder They Fall," *The Times* (London), September 15, 2001.

13 Steven Erlanger, "In Europe, Some Critics Say the Attacks Stemmed From American Failings," *New York Times,* September 22, 2001, p. B12.

14 Sarah Kershaw, "Renewed Outcry on Haitian Fugitive in Queens," *New York Times,* August 12, 2000, p. B2.

15 Edward W. Said, *Covering Islam: How the Media and the Experts Determine How We See the Rest of the World.* Updated and revised ed. (New York: Vintage, 1997), p. xii.

16 Jack G. Shaheen, *Reel Bad Arabs: How Hollywood Vilifies a People* (Northampton, Massachusetts: Interlink, 2001).

17 *The Sheik,* directed by George Melford (1921) and *Son of the Sheik,* directed by George Fitzmaurice (1926).

18 Said, *Covering Islam,* p. xi.

19 See David Rohde, "Militants in Kashmir Deny Pakistani Support," *New York Times,* September 22, 2002, p. 1: 27, and photograph on p. 1: 1.

20 Edward Alden, "Bush Offers Fresh Help to Pakistan," *Financial Times* (London), February 14, 2002, p. 10.

21 See Ahmad and Barsamian, *Eqbal Ahmad: Confronting Empire.*

22 See, among others, Philip Hitti, *History of the Arabs,* 10th rev. ed. (New York: Palgrave Macmillan, 2002). Albert Hourani, *A History of the Arab Peoples* (New York: Warner Books, 1992).

A Palestinian Perspective on the Conflict with Israel

KGNU, Boulder, Colorado, August 15, 2002

The crisis in Palestine might be the most severe in the thirty-five years of Israeli occupation. The Guardian in London reports "acute malnutrition" in Gaza.[1] What is your assessment of the situation?

It is dire. And it's almost entirely due to the Israeli occupation of West Bank cities. Gaza is fenced in like a giant cage. The roads between the cities are inaccessible to Palestinians. There is, however, a whole system of roads reserved for Israeli settlers who have illegally populated the West Bank and Gaza. If you include illegally annexed East Jerusalem, there are now more than 400,000 settlers. They are allowed to go around armed. Palestinians are basically confined to their homes for long stretches of curfew. The curfews are lifted for short periods of time so that they can go out and buy food. Most of the infrastructure of the West Bank now has been destroyed. Israel talks about "terrorist nests," but in fact they have nearly destroyed the civil infra-

134 **Culture and Resistance**

structure: Electricity, water, sanitation facilities, all the offices, not just of the Palestinian Authority, which Israel represents as a gang of terrorists, but which is also a civil authority. There are Ministries of Education, Labor, Planning, Central Bureau of Statistics, all of which are principally located in Ramallah. All of their buildings were destroyed. The computers were smashed and the hard drives and files were taken away by Israeli troops. A million schoolchildren's records were seized by the Israelis.[2] In addition, schools and universities are inaccessible to most students. They simply can't get through the roadblocks. And life, in the sense of trying to get from one place to another, is very difficult. To get, say, from Bir Zeit to the hospital in Ramallah—you can't. Or you are kept waiting at the roadblock for hours on end. Several dozen people have died because they could not get dialysis. The media, even in this country, are full of reports of people, mostly civilians, being shot at the checkpoints.

Of course, there is a great deal of media focus on suicide bombers. There are photos of the carnage and funerals with the names of victims. All these bombings are, of course, terrible incidents. But in almost every news report on almost every day from the West Bank and Gaza, if you look carefully at the end you will see that four, five, six Palestinians were killed. They are nameless. Killed for no particular reason. Lots of children have been killed. The rate of killing of Palestinians vs. Israelis is three, sometimes four, to one.[3]

A Palestinian Perspective on the Conflict with Israel 135

Malnutrition is the direct result of the Israelis preventing food from being distributed. So let's take something that just happened the other day. A truck from Gaza with 400 kilos of plums is trying to get through the cage. It is kept at a road-block for hours. The truck is in the sun. The fruit all rots.[4] The worst infractions have to do with the prevention of medical services, blood supplies, and medicine. I have a friend, a sick woman who had a permit to leave for medical reasons. She was being taken by ambulance from Ramallah to Amman, Jordan. She was sitting in the front. About 200 meters from the Qalandia checkpoint, the soldiers opened fire, destroying the windshield and missing her by several inches. That kind of thing is common.

I have just written an article entitled "Slow Death: Punishment by Detail."[5] That is what, I think, the Sharon plan is. To starve, beat down, and bring the Palestinians to their knees. He is not succeeding. Palestinians are staying on their land. They are not leaving. There is desperation and unhappiness but all the signs, as in all colonial wars, point to an upsurge of resilience and a will to resist.

There is no political horizon. Sharon's plan is basically to ask the U.S. for massive amounts of aid, which is a terrible ploy. He wants the aid and to keep the siege up. People talk about reform and there is a great deal of reform planned. Long before George Bush said that he thought we needed reform. What George Bush knows about Palestine can be engraved on the head of a pin. You can't have true reform or elections or security under the current conditions. Palestinians are con-

136   Culture and Resistance

fined to their homes. No one is allowed to circulate, and if you do, you are shot at. Cars are destroyed. The Israeli press is full of stories of the most wanton destruction, and now, really since April, the destruction of homes. Several thousand Palestinian homes have been destroyed in places like Jenin, Jabalya, and Deheishe by Caterpillar bulldozers supplied by the United States. The city center of the old city of Nablus has been invaded and is occupied by 150 Israeli tanks. We are talking about tiny, narrow streets. The tanks smash through the walls and the houses. They terrorize not terrorists but civilians.

To paraphrase the Israeli position: We don't have a negotiating partner. We take these measures in self-defense in response to Palestinian terrorism. How would you answer?

They had a negotiating partner for nine years since 1993, when Arafat and the PLO signed an agreement with them. During that time, and I've chronicled this in my books, the Israelis, who were suppose to vacate the West Bank and Gaza, conceded only 18 percent of the land to the Palestinians, which they have now reoccupied. And during that time, the number of settlements more than doubled in size. So as the so-called peace process was advancing and as negotiations were supposedly progressing, they were really going nowhere, the number of settlements and the amount of land taken from the Palestinians was greater and greater.

Since 1996, there have been a series of closures whereby Palestinians who depended on their livelihood for work in Is-

A Palestinian Perspective on the Conflict with Israel   137

rael were prevented from doing so. Israel has been importing tens of thousands of workers from countries like Romania and Thailand.[6] In Gaza alone, Palestinians are experiencing 70 percent unemployment, and nearly three-quarters of Palestinians are living on less then $2 a day.[7] There has been hunger and besiegement. All of this creates an atmosphere of desperation. People literally have to fight to live. Without an army, without an air force, without a leader, properly speaking, since Arafat has been imprisoned. And without any of the appurtenances of a civil authority, because Israel has destroyed them. That's the Palestinian situation. The Israelis then say there is no one to negotiate with. There is any number of Palestinians they could negotiate with. Most of the world, with the exception of the United States and Israel, is prepared to negotiate with the elected authority.

I myself am a dissenter and certainly would not vote for Arafat if there were elections. But he is now the elected leader of the Palestinians in an internationally monitored election in 1996. So there is somebody. But the whole purpose of Sharon and his government has been to delegitimize, brutalize, criminalize, isolate, and dehumanize the Palestinians so they can die like cockroaches. Their leaders, as Sharon said the other day, are treated as little more than a gang of assassins and corrupt terrorists.[8]

So yes, you can destroy any hope of an interlocutor, even though one remains, and say there is no one to negotiate with. About 80 percent of casualties on the Palestinian side have been civilians.[9] For almost a year, Israel has been carrying out

138   **Culture and Resistance**

what they call "targeted killings" or assassinations.[10] They finger some alleged leader and kill him either by a car bomb or helicopter missile or from an F-16. A couple of weeks ago, they did that to somebody they alleged was an important Hamas leader in Gaza. They killed him. But dropping a bomb from an F-16 into the most crowded place on earth—inevitably you are going to do some other damage. Four buildings were destroyed. Fifteen people were killed, nine of whom were children. Then Sharon says it is one of the most successful operations they've ever done.[11]

If killing nine children is a successful operation then one wonders why the attacks on Palestinians for their desperate suicide bombings doesn't also include condemnations of Israeli terror bombings, which are far greater. They have killed eighty people in these targeted assassinations.[12] No proof is ever adduced. No evidence given. They just say this is somebody who is plotting to do this, that, or the other thing, and we're going to kill him. And they kill him. And they kill everyone alongside him. If he is in a car, his family goes with him. And the Israelis are demolishing the houses of him and his family. Or the male members of his family are deported. In addition to that, since the reoccupation of the West Bank in the spring, Israel has detained numerous Palestinians, some of whom are now being held in Israel. That is illegal according to the Fourth Geneva Convention. You can't remove people from their land and take them to another country, which is what Israel has done. Some of them have been marked on their arms with ink, just as Jews were marked by the

A Palestinian Perspective on the Conflict with Israel   139

Nazis. Israel is a nuclear power, munificently equipped with the latest in American weaponry, facing a basically unarmed civilian population. That hardly qualifies as self-defense. In my opinion, it is terrorism and murder.

The issue, which is never looked at in the U.S. media, is not only these falsehoods about self-defense, but the occupation itself. It is never given as an issue over which Palestinians have been fighting and resisting for over thirty-five years. And the loss of their land. And the total failure of the Oslo peace process in which they lost even more land. The other thing that is never looked at is that Palestinians are a stateless people. Or that what Israel is doing is being done to a whole population, not just to individuals who are called terrorist. The purpose, as Sharon has more or less said, is to destroy the vestiges of Palestinian life. Either to make them leave in a mass transfer or ethnic cleansing, send them to Jordan, or see that they emigrate, run away, or die a slow death.

I think the Israeli argument about self-defense is rubbish. Were it not for the protection of the United States, which engages in similar practices elsewhere, it wouldn't stand up for a moment. Israel is the only country in the world that can get away with what it is doing in full view of TV. TV is imperfect of course. It does not provide background or context. But at least you can see the scenes of homes being destroyed and tanks moving into unarmed villages. To use words like self-defense for that is a travesty of language and preposterous in its claim.

140 Culture and Resistance

In what ways has the U.S. war on terrorism intersected with Israeli policies vis-à-vis the Palestinians?

It's been the greatest boon to Sharon. Routinely what he says is that what the United States is doing in Afghanistan in fighting bin Laden and al-Qaeda is what Israel is doing on the West Bank and Gaza.[13] Again, a preposterous comparison. The West Bank and Gaza are divided up into small districts in which Palestinians cannot move. They are locked in like sardines in a can. So the idea that there is some kind of terrorist central, as the United States says exists in Afghanistan, is not true of the West Bank and Gaza. That's number one.

Number two is that there has been an Israeli military occupation for thirty-five years. That's sort of overlooked, not because they don't want to admit there is an occupation but because they think the land is theirs. Just a couple of weeks ago, I saw Uzi Landau, the minister of the interior, on *The Charlie Rose Show* disputing the word occupation.[14] U.S. Defense Secretary Rumsfeld is now saying the same thing.[15] Landau said, How can you say occupation? We are going home. Even though there is another people there, it doesn't matter. Jews own the land by divine right.

Again, how preposterous an argument. Nobody, anywhere else in the world, would have the gall to try an argument like that. The third point is the dubious success of the war on terrorism is the same in the West Bank and Gaza and Afghanistan. Afghanistan is a ruined country. It has been bombed mercilessly. The United States claims it has captured

A Palestinian Perspective on the Conflict with Israel   141

or destroyed most of al-Qaeda. The United States is holding a couple of thousand prisoners. Some of them in illegal and inhumane conditions in Guantánamo Bay.[16] Originally, the United States attacked Afghanistan to get bin Laden. Bin Laden has disappeared. Mullah Omar is nowhere to be found. If anything, the country, despite the U.S.–supported Hamid Karzai regime, is in more turbulence than before.

I have no brief or interest in supporting the Taliban. They are horrible people. Recall that, in part, they were supported by the United States during the war against the Soviets and later during the civil war. They kept order, which is not the case now. If you wander around the streets of Kabul, and certainly beyond Kabul, you risk your life. The idea that terrorism can be fought and stopped is also preposterous because it is a metaphysical concept that has never been examined. It has turned the United States, like Israel, into a victim of some terrible almost theological evil which Bush and Sharon feel they are entitled as crusaders to fight by whatever means at their disposal. So morality, proportionality, attacks on civilians, all of that goes by the board.

The United States has now escalated, as Israel would like, to the proposition that it is entitled to change regimes. It openly says it wants to change regimes in Iraq, Palestine, and Iran. And so does Israel. There is an extraordinary coincidence between Israeli interests and American interests for the region. None of which, in my view, are justified by the real national interests of the United States. The hand of the Israeli lobby is very powerful here. And people like Richard Perle,

142   **Culture and Resistance**

Paul Wolfowitz, and Rumsfeld and all their minions are pushing this country into wars that are going to wreak havoc, not only on the region but on the economy of this country and indeed on the stability of the world itself.

There certainly is an Israeli lobby and it does have an influence on Congress and the executive branch. But there are other factors. Talk about U.S. geopolitical strategic interests in the Middle East.

Basically, there are two main pillars of U.S. foreign policy in the region. One is the security and strategic support of Israel as a U.S. surrogate. The other is assuring for itself the free flow of oil out of Saudi Arabia. You will notice in the media in the last six months that there has been a concerted campaign against Saudi Arabia and Egypt, the two main Arab allies of the United States. I don't think that is an accident. What is at stake is an Israeli-American desire to change the map of the Middle East so that the United States is in much more direct control of the oil reserves of the Gulf. And through setting up new compliant regimes, in these countries, like Iraq, they are going to be able to change these regimes to suit the Israeli desire to finish with its enemies.

Iraq is potentially the most powerful Arab state. It has oil. It has water. It has an educated population. It has a terrible government with a tyrant at the head of it. It has been decimated by sanctions for twelve years. And now the United States wants to go in and perhaps chop it up so that Iraq is no longer a viable Arab entity arrayed against Israel. The same is happening with Saudi Arabia. I have no brief for the House

A Palestinian Perspective on the Conflict with Israel 143

of Saud but they have been supplying the United States with cheap oil for sixty years at great sacrifice to their own people and the Arab world.

There is now a campaign against them. Perhaps to bring them down but at least to neutralize them so they cannot play a role in the common Arab struggle against the Israeli occupation. The same with Egypt. Both regimes are hopelessly corrupt, ineffective and tyrannical. They are one-party states. They suppress human rights. There is very little democracy. More in Egypt than Saudi Arabia. The point is to remove them, to neutralize them, as Iraq is going to be neutralized by this war. And at the same time to remove any strategic advantage to the Palestinians from these countries which have supported their struggle. The idea would be to demoralize and remove any support for the Palestinians. Neutralize and even remove Saudi Arabia by perhaps seizing the oil fields. Neutralizing Egypt. Destroying Iraq. Changing the regimes there and in Iran. And then you have a new map of the Middle East, which suits Israel perfectly.

Sharon has always thought in those terms. In 1982, he went into Lebanon, not just to destroy the PLO, which he did not do, but to change the government and install Bashir Gemayal, a compliant ally of Israel.[17] Gemayal was assassinated soon after he was inaugurated.[18] Sharon never seems to have learned his lesson. He still thinks that military power and United States support will enable him to redraw the map, in fact to play God. Unfortunately, he has in Bush and the Pentagon crowd willing allies who believe the same kind of non-

144 **Culture and Resistance**

sense. It is largely at an abstract and theoretical level. They know very little about the Middle East and the Islamic world.

The result is an enormous wave of anti-Americanism and resentment that this policy will in fact make worse. There are attempts now to establish a radio station and beam it to the Arabs to win them over to the United States and its ideas. Arabs are not fools. The American values that Bush keeps talking about exist perhaps in his mind and in the minds of a few people around him. But what Arabs, Muslims, and Europeans more and more see is a country that flouts international law. It tears up some treaties and refuses to sign others. It thinks of itself above and exceptional in all things. That's what people see, not American values, whatever they are. What we export from this country, aside from consumer goods, is something very different from the democracy and freedom the United States talks about. I think we are headed for really bad times.

In late July, University of Maryland professor Shibley Telhami told the Senate Foreign Relations Committee that "there is a pervasive resentment of the United States in the region."[19] If those assessments are correct, why then would the United States pursue policies that generate this kind of animosity and hostility?

That's a very interesting question. I think because there has been such a distortion in perception, largely because of Israel. The power of the Israeli lobby is such that it skews U.S. policy to give primacy to the well-being of Israel. That has now become fixed as a kind of permanent optic in U.S.

A Palestinian Perspective on the Conflict with Israel   145

policy. It is certainly the case in political discourse in this country. I'll give you an example. We are having a gubernatorial primary race in New York. Carl McCall is running for governor. He felt it imperative to validate himself by going to Israel. He went to a West Bank settlement and fired a rifle at "terrorists" to prove his loyalty to Israel and the sincerity of his support for Israel and its settlements.[20] That is routine. Hillary Clinton does the same kind of thing. Every senator and representative, with a few exceptions like Cynthia McKinney, will sign a letter saying we support Israel and we shouldn't impeach Sharon. That's built in.

Along with that is a tremendous popular ignorance about what the situation in the Middle East is like. The Arabs have never had a unified information policy. Arabs in the United States are a small minority compared to the much more powerful, much wealthier, and better-organized Jewish minority. Arabs are seen as terrorists and fanatics. Islam is characterized as a violent religion. And of course the events of the last few years have reinforced that. You're not allowed to explain any of this. It has now been forced on us by former leftists like Christopher Hitchens, Michael Ignatieff, and Michael Walzer, who have come aboard in this extraordinary campaign to show that Islamic terrorism is a free-standing thing. It's lodged at the very heart of Islam. "Islamo-fascism."[21] They propagate this line. With the result that dissent and rational discussion have been virtually banned.

You can't find anything in the media to rebut these absurd claims. Then you have people like Dennis Ross, the for-

146   **Culture and Resistance**

mer Middle East peace negotiator during the Clinton administration. He was a paid member of the Israeli lobby before he took up his position and now again since he left. He comes on TV and says the Arabs turned down all these wonderful offers the Israelis made. Israel is a peace-loving state. Therefore, the Arabs are delinquent and this is a part of the world we ought to nuke. Especially with the rage and anger, understandable, after 9/11, the media suggests that, yes, that is in fact what should be done.

The fact that there are 280 million Arabs and 1.3 billion Muslims in the world, and not all of them are the same, and not all of them are terrorists, all that gets forgotten. And you find yourself in this world of abstractions and generalizations which are consolidated by so-called distinguished orientalists like Bernard Lewis and others, who say the whole world of Islam has gone wrong.[22] It's as if Lewis is talking about children in a nursery who misbehave and ought to be put into reform school. The result is that a rational discussion of U.S. interests is impossible. If you try, you are accused of anti-Semitism. But most of the time you can't even get the time and space to argue this point of view. There is also great apathy in a public for whom the Middle East is a distant place that is full of terrorists and people who want to kill us. So we drift into more wars, more destruction and more anti-Americanism.

In his introduction to The Pen and the Sword, *Eqbal Ahmad wrote, "Palestinians have the misfortune of being oppressed by a rare*

A Palestinian Perspective on the Conflict with Israel 147

adversary, a people who themselves have suffered long and deeply from persecution."[23]

As I have often said, we are the victims of the victims. Israel was founded in the aftermath of World War II and the Holocaust. There was a Zionist movement that began in the 1890s and there were settlements in Palestine well before WWII. There was Jewish terrorism against the British who held the mandate for Palestine. All of that is forgotten. What people remember, and correctly to some degree, is the Jews of Europe had no place to go after the war. The Europeans didn't want them, nor did the Americans. They played, in my view, into the hands of the Zionists like Ben-Gurion who took them to Palestine, and in the process displaced and dispossessed an entire people.

It wasn't an empty country. People were already there; a population of 800,000 was driven out in 1948. We now know this from the Israeli military archives. Israel for the past fifty-four years has benefited from the halo of European, Christian, and American guilt as to what happened to Jews in Europe. Unfortunately, Palestinians have paid the price. We are always seen as anti-Jewish. There is the refrain of killing Jewish children, while we are really unable to do anything against one of the most powerful military juggernauts in the world. So it's OK to kill Palestinians because they are in some way continuing the Nazi tradition. Israeli Prime Minister Begin said precisely that in 1982 when his armies invaded Lebanon.[24]

148　　　　　　**Culture and Resistance**

Then there is the moral obligation. Take Germany. It is in a tough position because the Holocaust was a German phenomenon. Its relationship with Israel is extremely sensitive. Nevertheless, courage requires both Germany and Britain, the architects of the Palestinian tragedy, to face up to their responsibility. When the Germans committed the Holocaust, and when the British left Palestine to the Zionists, they created tragedy for the Palestinians. It is a very difficult minefield to negotiate. But it does seem, to me at least, that, shining through it all, there is a clear case for moral justice on the Palestinian side. Many of us say, why should we pay the bills that Europe imposed on us for what they did to the Jews? Historically, Jews in Arab and Islamic countries have had a much better time than in Christian countries. There is a long history of Jewish communities throughout the Middle East going back to the days of early Christianity. There were communities in places like Iraq, Yemen, and Egypt. They felt themselves to be part of those countries. There was no important movement from these countries to go to Palestine to establish a Jewish state. They felt themselves to be part of the Middle Eastern mix of many races and religions.

What has happened is the Middle East has been transformed into a region pursuing mythological racial purity. So that Israel is fighting and killing Palestinians in the interest of preserving the Jewish character of the state. In my opinion, the only solution is to say that this is a land for two peoples, in which two peoples in fact exist, and the only hope is that they coexist in equality and not one exist as the subordinate or the

A Palestinian Perspective on the Conflict with Israel 149

subaltern class for the other. But as I say, so powerful is the claim of Jews upon the conscience of the West that it is difficult for us Palestinians to oppose this in the name of our rights, our dispossession, and our displacement.

But it is happening. More and more people over time are recognizing that the actions of Israel cannot be justified by frequent references to the Holocaust. True, Israel is an independent state. But, it is still the only state in the world that has never declared its boundaries. There are armistice lines. Israel reserves the right for itself to expand, to take over more territory, to throw out more people. That has nothing to do with the Holocaust. It is messianic zealotry of the kind that is very dangerous. It is simply going to perpetuate a very bloody outcome. Many Israelis have on their own figured out that this is a suicidal policy. Because no matter what Israel does to the Palestinians—let's assume they kill them or get them all out—they are still going to be surrounded by hostile Arab states. Their hostility is increasing daily by the scenes that are now routinely seen on Arab, indeed, on world, television. The Israelis are laying up a store of resentment and even hatred that is going to endure for generations. Their policy is very shortsighted. They cannot assume that the United States is going to support them forever. And that the rest of the world is going to let them get away flouting international law and UN resolutions. At some point the reckoning is going to come.

There are a couple of other factors shaping and influencing U.S. Middle East policy that I'd like you to comment on. One is the giant

150   **Culture and Resistance**

U.S. military contractors like Lockheed Martin, Boeing, and Northrop Grumman that are clearly interested in the region being kept in a state of turmoil and conflict in order to sell more and more weaponry. The other is the enthusiasm of elements of the Christian right for Israeli policies.

Take the first one. It is a terribly important factor. I think that almost every one of the 500 congressional districts in this country has a defense industry of some sort. The selling of arms abroad, which is a major U.S. export, has now become a jobs issue not a defense issue. That's on the one hand. On the other, the Middle East spends more on arms than any other area in the world. Saudi Arabia is one of the largest purchasers of U.S. arms.[25] There is a kind of dependence, which is overlooked by those who campaign against Saudi Arabia. Saudi Arabia, the United Arab Emirates, Kuwait, and Qatar are buying the most advanced fighter planes and laser guided missiles but are unable to use them. It's really an irony.

Also, the Egyptian army, which is the largest single employer in Egypt, is heavily supplied by the United States. The arms are useless. They distort the structure of the economy and are bought at the expense of the welfare of the people. Expenditures on education, public health, technology transfer, and other things are severely limited by these arms supplies which are really done at the behest of the United States for the benefit of corporations such as the ones you mentioned. And what it does, certainly in the case of Israel, Egypt, and the other countries is to militarize the area. So there is always an idle and too large military class, which in the case of

A Palestinian Perspective on the Conflict with Israel 151

Egypt represses the population. The Egyptians seem to be unwilling to go to war or to go to peace. And, in the case of Israel, they are supplied with the most advanced weapons, which they readily use against Palestinian civilians.

There is now, I'm happy to report, a growing divestment movement on U.S. campuses, requiring that universities divest themselves from some of these companies that do military business with Israel.[26] This movement, which is growing amazingly, is following the pattern of the anti-apartheid movement in South Africa in the 1970s and 1980s. Take Caterpillar. I have a particular bone to pick with Caterpillar because it is their bulldozers which are used to destroy Palestinian homes, sometimes with the people inside them. Companies like that are now coming under public scrutiny, drawing attention to this unholy feeding of the military fires in the Middle East, which of course benefits U.S. corporations. It also, in a kind of indirect way, increases U.S. hegemony. That is the idea. Because with the arms go the spare parts, the trainers, and so on. It increases the obligation of the Saudis on the Americans who then can station more forces.

And the Christian right?

There is a great irony in people like Pat Robertson, Jerry Falwell, and others who openly advocate support for Israel to the nth degree. To the degree of saying Palestinians are killers, Muslims are renegades, atheists, and violent fanatics. But if you look carefully at it—and I've studied it because my family house in Jerusalem is now occupied by something

152   **Culture and Resistance**

called the International Christian Embassy; it is one of the more far out Christian fundamentalist groups, principally American—the plan behind all of these groups is deeply anti-Semitic. They support Israel. But in what sense? They say Israel is the country of the Jews. It was given to them by God. Jews should go there in larger and larger numbers. That is exactly the Zionist dream. That the diaspora should end and that all Jews should return to Zion.

But the Christian Right continues further and says that, in order for the Messiah to come, the Jews all have to be in Palestine. The Second Coming would then include a great war in which all the Jews who don't convert to Christianity will be killed. And the new age of the world will begin. So at the back of this extraordinary interest in Israel is a deeply and radically anti-Semitic goal, which is to destroy the Jews, once they have all gathered in Zion. There is a marriage of convenience between the Christian Right and the Republican Right. A very large percentage of the population of the South and Western United States, seventy to eighty million people, regard George Bush as their leader. His policies, which are very anti-Palestinian and manifest no understanding of the suffering of the Palestinians, are backed to the hilt by these people, whose interests he serves, as well as the Israeli lobby, which has been steadily turning rightward toward precisely the enemy it had perceived in the 1970s and 1980s. They've now gone over to the other side and espouse and help in propaganda and financing the Christian Right. The

A Palestinian Perspective on the Conflict with Israel   **153**

word distortion comes to mind immediately to characterize this. It has become grotesque.

Again returning to Eqbal Ahmad, your very close friend. He died in Pakistan in 1999. In 1998 he said that "Osama bin Laden is a sign of things to come." I asked him to explain what he meant. He said, "The United States has sowed in the Middle East and in South Asia very poisonous seeds. These seeds are growing now. Some have ripened, and others are ripening. An examination of why they were sown, what has grown, and how they should be reaped is needed. Missiles won't solve the problem."[27] What would solve the problem?

I think one has to be quite pessimistic about it. The United States is not simply a collection of individuals like Bush or Rumsfeld. And if we say, they should go and be replaced by more understanding people, it is not enough. It is a system. It is a whole outlook. The citizenry should become more aware and more informed, especially as we seem now to be entering an even more aggressive phase with the projected war for regime change in Iraq. I think what needs to be done is to widen awareness of what the stakes are in the Middle East, and for the first time to recognize that the Middle East is not simply a collection of Muslim fundamentalists.

In every major Arab country, there is a human rights movement. There are movements for freedom of information and freedom of expression. There is a remarkably burgeoning women's movement. The increase in the number of socially active women in the last ten years has been quite dramatic. There is a liberal culture in countries like Egypt. And

154 Culture and Resistance

even in Kuwait, there is a liberal culture struggling against the Islamists. But also against the tyranny of one party, oligarchical, or one-family rule. So there are these contests. What we don't have is a dynamic awareness of the dialectic of this struggle. We must see it for what it is, and position ourselves to be part of that debate, say between American intellectuals and Arab and Muslim intellectuals, instead of one preaching at the other and hating the other.

I don't want to give myself as an example but I belong to both worlds. I've always found it possible to coexist between the two worlds, because there are like-minded people in both worlds who want coexistence, who believe in rational argument, who believe in a secular rather than a religious politics, and who think that force, militarization, and repression have been so counterproductive as to be eschewed and avoided at any cost. I am now at the point where, although I am not a pacifist, I am willing to advocate pacifism because immediately so much would fall away. The armies are useless. And when they are useful, as in the case of Israel and the United States, they create more destruction and sow the seeds of more dissension for generations to come. I feel there are a lot of people who are willing to listen to this message both in the Arab world and the United States. The problem has been, How do you get these people to meet and understand each other given the drum beating of the media and the obduracy of the government with its institutions?

I think there is a hope in civil society through the churches, universities, the places where there is relative freedom to dis-

A Palestinian Perspective on the Conflict with Israel   155

cuss. More people of the generation after mine are beginning to be aware of this. That is the only hope for change. I don't think it can come from coups or regime change of the kind the Bush administration is talking about.

Notes

1   Jonathan Steele, "For Hire: The Boy Human Shields in Gaza's Most Desperate Town," *The Guardian* (London), August 6, 2002, p. 2.
2   See Ewen MacAskill, "Schools, Banks, and a Puppet Theatre Trashed," *The Guardian* (London), April 26, 2002, p. 13.
3   See chapter 2, note 5.
4   See Joshua Hammer, "Road Rage and the Intifada," *Newsweek,* July 30, 2001, p. 20.
5   See Edward W. Said, "Punishment by Detail," *Al-Ahram Weekly* 598 (August 8–14, 2002). Online at http://www.ahram.org.eg/weekly/2002/598/op2.htm.
6   Tal Muscal, "Foreign Worker Permits Continue to Rise Despite Government Decision," *Jerusalem Post*, December 19, 2002, p. 11.
7   Khaled Abu Toameh and Melissa Radler, "Palestinian Society Teetering on Edge of Ruin, UNRWA Warns," *Jersualem Post*, December 12, 2002, p. 2, Wilkinson, "Palestinian Towns Wobbling on Last Legs."
8   Ramit Plushnick-Masti, "Sharon Calls Palestinian Authority a 'Terror Posse,'" Associated Press, August 8, 2002.
9   See chapter 2, note 5.
10 See Dan Izenberg, "Report Slams 'Assassination' Policy," *Jerusalem Post,* October 17, 2002, p. 3, referencing reports by the Public Committee Against Torture in Israel (PCATI) and the Palestinian Society for the Protection of Human Rights and the Environment (LAW).

156   **Culture and Resistance**

11 Sharon called the assassination of Salah Shehada a "great success." Suzanne Goldenberg, Brian Whitaker, and Nicholas Watt, "Sharon Hails Raid as Great Success," *The Guardian* (London), July 24, 2002, p. 1; Anton La Guardia, "Israel Divided by Policy of 'Target Killing,'" *Daily Telegraph* (London), July 26, 2002, p. 16.

12 See chapter 2, note 5.

13 See Gary Younge, "Lots of Wars on Terror: The Bush Doctrine Is Now a Template for Conflicts Worldwide," *The Guardian* (London), December 10, 2001, p. 17.

14 Interview with Uzi Landau, *The Charlie Rose Show*, PBS, June 28, 2002.

15 Rumsfeld referred to the "so-called occupation" of Palestinian land. Barbara Slavin, "Rumsfeld View Veers from Mideast Policy," *USA Today,* August 7, 2002, p. 10A.

16 See Julian Borger, "Civil Liberties Clampdown: Rights Flouted at Guantanamo Bay," *The Guardian* (London), September 9, 2002, p. 4.

17 Robert Fisk, *Pity the Nation: Lebanon at War*, 3rd ed. (London: Oxford University Press, 2001), p. 274.

18 Fisk, *Pity the Nation,* pp. 353–55.

19 Shibley Telhami, Testimony, Senate Foreign Relations Committee, Washington, D.C., Federal News Service, July 31, 2002.

20 See Adam Nagourney, "McCall's Israel Trip Lingers As Issue in Governor's Race," *New York Times*, March 13, 2002, p. B5; Susan Saulny, "Demonstrations Highlight Deep Divisions Over Growing Conflict in Middle East," *New York Times,* April 6, 2002, p. B5.

21 See Oliver Burkeman, "Nation Loses its Voice," *The Guardian* (London), September 30, 2002, p. 7.

22 Bernard Lewis, *What Went Wrong? Western Impact and Middle Eastern Response* (New York: Oxford University Press, 2002). See Edward W. Said, "Impossible Histories: Why the Many Islams Cannot be Simplified" (review of Bernard Lewis' *What Went Wrong? Western Impact and Middle Eastern Response* and Karen Armstrong's *Islam: A Short History*), *Harper's Magazine*, July 2002.

A Palestinian Perspective on the Conflict with Israel   157

23 Eqbal Ahmad, Introduction, in Edward W. Said, *The Pen and the Sword: Conversations with David Barsamian* (Monroe, Maine: Common Courage Press, 1994), p. 15.

24 See Edward Cody, "'Soldier' or 'Terrorist'; Through a Mideast Looking Glass," *Washington Post*, July 7, 1982, p. A1.

25 See chapter 2, note 36.

26 See Matthew MacLean, "Students Demand Divestment, This Time Targeting Israel," *Christian Science Monitor*, April 9, 2002, p. 14.

27 Ahmad, *Eqbal Ahmad,* p. 135.

At the Rendezvous of Victory

New York, New York, February 25, 2003

What role can culture play in resistance movements?

Take the Palestinian situation as a case in point. There's a whole assembly of cultural expression that has become part of the consolidation and persistence of Palestinian identity. There's a Palestinian cinema, a Palestinian theater, a Palestinian poetry, and literature in general. There's a Palestinian critical and political discourse. In the case of a political identity that's being threatened, culture is a way of fighting against extinction and obliteration. Culture is a form of memory against effacement. In that respect, I think it's terribly important.

But there is a another dimension of cultural discourse—the power to analyze, to get past cliché and straight out-and-out lies from authority, the questioning of authority, the search for alternatives. These are also part of the arsenal of cultural resistance.

160　　　　　　**Culture and Resistance**

Culture can pose a threat to power. I'm thinking about the invasion of Beirut in 1982, led by Ariel Sharon, in which offices holding Palestinian archives were wrecked and destroyed. Twenty years later, another Sharon-led invasion of Ramallah ransacked the Khalil Sakakini Cultural Center.[1]

What you're pointing to is actually very important. The Khalil Sakakeeny Cultural Center is named after a man who was a principal educator of Palestine before 1948. He happened to be a friend of my family's. As a boy, I used to see him come to my family's house. He was famous for a school that he ran, to which many of the nationalist bourgeoisie went. It was not part of the mandatory system. It was not an English school. It was a national school. It was nonsectarian. And it taught young Palestinian men the understanding of their cultural and political heritage. Sakakini himself was Christian. But many of his most famous students were Muslim. It was an important crucible of nationalist consciousness as a school. So the center in Ramallah, which is named for him, is a symbol of Palestinian national, intellectual, and cultural life, and therefore is a target for the Israelis.

In 2002, they carted off the Palestinian Central Bureau of Statistics. They took away all the computers, destroyed the hard drives, and actual files were taken, as they belonged to the Ministry of Education and the Ministry of Health.[2] Anything that resembles an archive that gives material existence to a history is thought of as something to be destroyed. That is the folly of every imperial conqueror. Certainly in the colo-

At the Rendezvous of Victory   161

nial context, as in Algeria, the French sought to prevent Arabic being taught in the schools. But people will find other places—in this case, the mosque—to learn Arabic and perpetuate the oral tradition. There's always an attempt at repression and there's always a popular ingenuity and will that resists.

Mahmoud Darwish is considered Palestine's national poet. What is his importance?

It's complicated. Darwish, first of all, grew up in Israel. He was not a Palestinian like most of the members of the PLO. He wasn't from the diaspora. He remained and became an Israeli citizen. He is fluent in Hebrew, as well as Arabic. He is known as one of the earliest of the so-called resistance poets. That is to say, he spoke about nationalist themes and, above all, the affirmation of Palestinian identity. His most famous poem is entitled, "Identity Card," which begins "Record! I am an Arab."[3] It's a poem that actually derives from the personal experience of having to register at an Israeli office. Until 1966, the Palestinians inside Israel were under military rule, so they had to report constantly, to register. So he, in a kind of defiant way, tells the man, "Record that I am an Arab." That almost inadvertently became the first line of a poem.

Later, when Darwish left Palestine in the early 1970s and lived in Egypt and later in Beirut and Paris, he was a poet of exile. Certainly I think along with the recently deceased Syrian poet Nizar Qabbani and the still contemporary and writing Syrian poet Adonis, Darwish is really one of the great poets of the Arab world. He is very much like Faiz Ahmed Faiz was in the South Asian tradition. Darwish draws enormous crowds, in the thousands, who come to hear him recite his poetry.

He's a voracious reader, and despite his long affiliation with the PLO, he is a rather reclusive man, rarely taking public positions. He's quite cosmopolitan in his tastes and outlook. Over the last twenty years, in which he's been enormously productive, he's developed another style of poetry, which I would call meditative and lyrical. He's written about poetry ranging from topics about Andalusia, to the Native Americans, to his serious illness, to, most recently, his last great ode—*qasida* is the Arabic word—called "Under Siege."[4] The poem is an account of being besieged during the Israeli invasion of the West Bank in the spring of 2002.

He's a poet of many dimensions. He's certainly a public poet, but also an intensely personal and lyrical poet. And I think, on the world scale today, he's certainly one of the best. He ranks with Derek Wolcott and Seamus Heaney—to mention two Nobel Prize winners, one from the Caribbean, one from Ireland—in mastery of his language. He manages to amalgamate a great deal of imagery from the Arabic Koranic tradition, in a secular way. He's not a religious poet at all, but many of his poems are inflected with the language of the Koran and of the Gospels. He is also influenced by Lorca, Neruda, and Yevtushenko. He spent some time in Russia, so he's quite familiar with that literary tradition, as well as with some of the newer poets such as Brodsky.

At the Rendezvous of Victory 163

You've compared Darwish with W.B. Yeats's early period.

Yes, because he has been very much associated with the struggle for liberation, the way Yeats was in the struggle for Irish freedom against British colonialism. Yeats was always associated with formal efforts at cultural life, for example the Abbey Theatre. He was a member of the Irish parliament. He was more of a public figure than Darwish has been, although Darwish is very well-known. But he has never had a formal position other than for the period he served on the Palestinian National Council, which doesn't mean very much.

What's the line between art and polemic? Can they be too tightly interwoven? For example, take Pablo Neruda. He made his fame as a romantic and metaphysical poet. But then he went to Spain during the Civil War and his poetry took a dramatic turn. He wrote, "I'm Explaining a Few Things" in response to his critics, who asked "Where are the lilacs?" And he writes, "And you will ask: why doesn't his poetry / speak of dreams and leaves / and the great volcanoes of his native land?" He beckons the reader three times at the conclusion of this poem, "Come and see the blood in the streets."[5]

Well, in the case of the Palestinian poet, for example, today, like Neruda, he is—or she is, because there are very fine women poets, like Fadalla Tukan—answering to the needs of the situation. And the situation for us, since 1948, has been heavily political, in the sense that our self-expression as a people has been blocked. So since every poet in a way answers to the political and historical needs of the time in some way—even, as Adorno says, in the case of the lyric, which is the most private of all forms—there is an implicit relationship to the political, even in the most nonpolitical of all forms, a relation of negativity. But in the poetry of Palestine and of the Arab world, there are interesting reasons for the political engagement that you find in literature—which doesn't make it simply polemical. There is polemical literature without artistic merit. But there is no necessary contradiction between aesthetic merit and political themes.

In the Arab and specifically the Palestinian case, aesthetics and politics are intertwined, for a number of reasons. One is the ever-present repression and blockage of life, on every level, by the Israeli occupation, by the dispossession of an entire nation, and the sense that we are a nation of exiles. So that defines our situation, to which the writer responds. Another dynamic is the pressure of the Islamic and Arabic language tradition itself, which is very powerful. Language is the central cultural expression of the Arabs. It is very closely tied to—in fact, is—the language of God, as in the Koran. The Koran is *munzal.* It descended directly from God. It's the unmediated word of God. So the poet, at a time of revolutionary change and resistance, is also trying to find a voice for herself or himself within this tradition. Adonis perfectly expresses that in his poetry, and that's what makes it so difficult to understand. It is a poetry of extraordinary knowledge, and counter-knowledge at the same time. He feels that he has to create a new language, fighting against the old language, while drawing on the same tradition of Koranic idiom and belief.

At the Rendezvous of Victory   165

All that many Americans know about Arabic is the myth that there are a thousand words for knife.

Yes, that's ridiculous. Arabic is terribly misrepresented. It's thought of as being first of all a controversial language because it is the language of Islam. And it's considered to be a violent language. But in fact, for somebody like myself, who knows a lot of languages, it's the most beautiful of languages. It's very symmetrical in its structure and logical. Arabic has a very Aristotelian structure.

You must wince when you hear Colin Powell speaking about Iraq at the United Nations and saying "Sodom" repeatedly. What's that about? You don't have to know Arabic to be able to say "Saddam."

It's a form of arrogance and obviously of contempt. I think there's an attempt on the one hand to demonize, and trivialize him, and on the other hand to show that familiarity breeds contempt. That Iraq is really nothing more than this man, whose name is always mispronounced, as you said. Of course, he is an awful dictator, but in the class of dictators the world over, historically, let's say in the twentieth century, he is pretty small fish.

What we're talking about extends way beyond Colin Powell, to multimillion-dollar paid news anchors who say I-raq, I-ran, muhdrassas, *the* shuhreeyah, *the* Mooslems, *and* Izlum.

Yes, it's all part of the same arsenal of Orientalist clichés that are designed to alienate, distance, and dehumanize a peo-

166   **Culture and Resistance**

ple, which is what has happened to us. That's why most Arabs feel tremendous animosity toward the U.S. media and government. The prevailing public discourse is so ignorant and at the same time so familiar in its contempt for these central things in our lives that we see it as a kind of assault on our culture and our civilization.

Returning to the issue of poetry, Laura Bush planned a celebration of Walt Whitman, Emily Dickenson, and Langston Hughes at the White House on February 12. She canceled the event rather abruptly when she learned that some of the poets planned to express opposition to war in Iraq.[6]

It's absolutely clear that if any poet would have gone, it would have been a disgrace, because it was a shameless and naked effort on the part of the White House to give itself the authority of culture, as is so often done in this country, to neutralize it and give it a kind of decorative status, rather than an engaged one. And I'm very glad she had the good sense to cancel it, rather than trying to bring a few poets in who would stand there pretending that Whitman and Dickenson had nothing to do with the war. The whole issue of authority and power was being raised by Laura Bush's effort to bring these poets to the White House. The fact that some poets had openly said they were not going was the right thing to do, and I'm glad the whole thing fell through.

And there have subsequently been counter-readings all over the country.

It shows the deep unpopularity of this war, and above all, the sense that we're entering a unique stage in our history as Americans. The government is in the hands of a cabal. I think we can talk about a regime here, or a junta, and not a government that's democratically elected and representative in the true sense of the word. The Democratic Party doesn't exist as an alternative force. The Bush administration is dominated by a group of military-minded neoconservatives who are fanatically pro-Israel. They are determined to prosecute this war against Iraq, not for reasons having anything to do with American security, but rather, as they have said, for assuring world dominance for the United States, no matter what it costs, in terms of blood and treasure, no matter what damage is done to the rest of the world. Hence the recourse to poetry as an alternative form of expression.

Ralph Nader and others have called this group—George Bush, Dick Cheney, Paul Wolfowitz, Richard Perle—"chicken hawks."

That's right, because none of them served in the military, though all of them had a chance. Bush was actually commissioned, but went AWOL for about a year, when he was in the Texas National Guard in the mid-1970s.[7] So it's disgraceful that these people who have no experience of war are the ones proselytizing for war.

168   **Culture and Resistance**

This group also says it wants to bring democracy to the Middle East.

They are trivializing the notion of democracy by proclaiming that that is what they are trying to do in the Middle East. I don't think it's ever happened in history that democracy is brought in by conquest and bombing, which this war is going to entail. One wonders where these perverted ideas come from.

I'm very pleased that there is so much in the way of ferment and demonstrations against the war on Iraq. But I'm surprised that there isn't more outrage, given that this war goes against the interests and indeed the well-being of this country, in terms of its cost, the damage that's going to be done, and the sheer immorality of it. It's a wonder that they've gotten away with this as long as they have.

On February 15, there were as many as a half a million people in the streets of New York. The next day, there may have been 200,000 in San Francisco.[8] This is an unprecedented outpouring of opposition before a war starts.

I agree with you. It shows that there may be an emerging critical sense, as a result, ironically, of September 11. This sense that we are vulnerable and that we belong as a nation and a people to world history and world politics. People are going beyond the panaceas and formulas—the idea that people hate us because of our democracy and our values and our freedom—to an understanding that maybe there's reason for being critical of America. And being critical of our interventions abroad, our overweening power, our wish to demonstrate over and over again that we can do anything we want. We contravene accords. We are defiant of the United Nations. And I hope that people will also become aware of how some American allies, like Israel, participate in the same kind of lawlessness. When Bush keeps saying that now is the time for the United Nations to demonstrate that it's serious about its resolutions on Iraq, we have to ask: What about the many more UN resolutions that have been flouted by Israel and the United States? Palestinians are being killed on a daily basis in contravention of the Geneva Conventions, the UN Charter, and numerous UN resolutions. I think that kind of hypocrisy is beginning to be more widely understood.

There is a gap, not only in Europe, but in the United States, between the palace and public opinion.

Absolutely. Everywhere. I would say in most countries, with few exceptions, there is a tremendous gap between the will of the large mass of the people and their supposed representatives. I think we are on the edge of a breakdown in what could be called representative democracy. It doesn't seem to obtain anywhere. Certainly, it's not the case in England or Italy. It's certainly not true in many of the Arab countries that the government is representative of the people.

Arab public opinion is often reduced to something called "the street." It was interesting to note when three million Italians turned out

170   **Culture and Resistance**

in Rome and perhaps two million protested in Britain, the marchers were not called "the street." [9]

Let me tell you something about the word "street." It's used a great deal by Orientalists. There's a kind of unconscious identification between the word "street" in connection with the Arabs, and the late nineteenth and early twentieth century usage of the term "street Arab." Street Arabs are vagrants. A lot of Victorian writing refers to people on the street, what we would call "street people." Peddlers, panhandlers, and the like are frequently referred to as "street Arabs." So I think referring to the "Arab street" in this way suggests that these are riff-raff, the kind of unimportant flotsam and jetsam of a society which is basically made up of barbarians and subhuman people. I think it's not an accident that this term is always used to talk about Arab public opinion.

In fact, Arab political discussions are more subtle and represent a wider spectrum of opinion than in the United States. Al-Jazeera, the satellite television network based in Qatar, is a good example. Non-state owned television is more self-critical in the Arab world than in the United States. The U.S. media, as you have written, is going through one of its worst moments. [10] Television in the United States considers itself to be an arm of the government as it mobilizes for war.

Let's talk more about the weakening of democracy. Ten million people turned out on the weekend of February 15, and were dismissed by

At the Rendezvous of Victory 171

George Bush as a "focus group."[11] This must have been the largest focus group in history.

Yes, it certainly was. But it also shows the dismissive and incredibly insular attitude of the president, who really thinks—from everything I've read about him—that he communicates with God. That really is a function of monotheistic fundamentalism. It has, alas, many resonances for me. One side of my family was fundamentalist Baptist. In this worldview, God speaks directly to the human being and therefore that person brooks no argument and is utterly convinced of his being right. It's not at all limited to Islam. You find it in Judaism. It's very much a part of the Puritan and Protestant tradition, and I suppose in some ways it's also part of the Catholic tradition. But it's particularly despicable and dangerous when this view is held by the president of the most powerful country in the world.

One of the things that is constantly occluded from any discussion about Iraq is that it also happens to be the home of three of the oldest Christian communities in the world—the Chaldeans, the Assyrians, and the Armenians. Judaism, Christianity, and Islam all trace their origin to Abraham, who was born in Ur, in southern Iraq.

It's a matter of some concern to me that almost no attention is paid to Iraq as the cultural center of the entire Arab world and indeed of Muslim civilization. Iraq's is an unbroken civilization that goes back millennia to Sumeria, Assyria, and Babylon. But it's all been reduced to "Sodom," as you

172   **Culture and Resistance**

point out. Don't forget that Iraq was the seat of the Abbasid caliphate, which is the high point of Arab civilization. Iraq today is still vital to Arab culture. There's a saying that the Egyptians write, the Lebanese publish, and the Iraqis read. Baghdad is certainly the art capital of the Arab world. And of all the Arab countries, Iraq is the most well endowed with natural and human resources. It possesses a great deal of water and oil. It has a highly developed middle and professional class, which has been badly weakened by the sanctions. There's no awareness of who the great figures in Iraqi culture are—the great writers, artists, painters, sculptors, and scientists. It's just another sign of the chasm that exists between the Islamic Arab world, on the one hand, and the West, on the other.

Iraq is also where writing was invented.

Indeed, and it's very much in the consciousness of every Arab, especially now, as Iraq is about to be attacked. I think it's true to say that there is no love anywhere in the Arab world for Saddam Hussein. But there is concern for the long-suffering people of Iraq, who have had to bear the twelve years of sanctions and depredations, as well as continued bombing, malnutrition, hunger, ill health, deprivation of school supplies and books, and so on. All of that is profoundly felt in the Arab world. Bush says "We have no quarrel with the Iraqi people," and the next thing you know, there are 6,000 cruise missiles headed for Baghdad, so obviously there's a contradiction there.[12]

At the Rendezvous of Victory

In a "Shock and Awe" attack that can only evoke Blitzkrieg in people's memories.[13]

That's the idea. Like Dresden or Hiroshima, the attack is supposed to have a terrifying and paralyzing effect on the population.

You pay careful attention to the use of language. Language is manipulated to create misunderstanding. Two examples. One from the New York Times: *"Most Palestinians consider settlers and soldiers in the West Bank to be the vanguard of an illegal occupation."*[14] *That's one. Another common media refrain is the comment that "Baghdad claims that the US-led sanctions are leading to mass malnutrition and unusually high rates of infant mortality."*[15]

I must tell you with sadness about the use of these words "alleged" and "claimed" that are now so prevalently used when describing Arab suffering. Last fall, I associated myself with a group of Columbia University faculty to address the president of the university to discuss a plan for Columbia to divest itself of stocks in companies engaged in military contracts with Israel. And then we went on to talk about human rights abuses, the bombing and bulldozing of Palestinian homes, in addition to the creation of an apartheid system. His response was to say that the comparison between what Israel is doing now and South African apartheid is outrageous and offensive. And he referred to "alleged" human rights abuses. This is after reams of reports by Amnesty International, Human Rights Watch, B'Tselem, and the United Nations. So

174 **Culture and Resistance**

that's a common tactic. Arabs exaggerate. The claims of Arab suffering are yet to be documented, no matter how much they suffer. It's very much in common parlance now, and it's part of the same propaganda apparatus that demeans people and dehumanizes them.

Another tactic is to say about Palestinians that they don't feel the same things we do. They don't have the same values we do. They don't understand human life the way we do. That was one of the classical arguments of colonialism, beginning in the eighteenth century. The idea that so-called underdeveloped people don't appreciate, don't know how to use the land, and therefore European settlers deserve to take the land from them. That was the argument made in this country. It was made in Africa. It was made in India. And the Zionists used the same language in Palestine when they came during the early part of the twentieth century. They talked about "redeeming" the land from the people who lived there, who are always described as Bedouin and nomadic.

In 2002, a fairly well-known poet, Tom Paulin, was invited to speak at Harvard University. There was an enormous amount of controversy around his invitation because he had been very critical of Israel.[16]

It's a complicated story, because it goes back further than the Tom Paulin incident. It goes back to Harvard President Lawrence Summers's response earlier in the year to the divestment campaign. Summers gave a lecture—or was it a sermon?—in the main church at Harvard about the emer-

At the Rendezvous of Victory

gence of anti-Semitism. He used as his main example the fact that there was this rising criticism of Israel, most recently by faculty members, all over the country. A divestment campaign began at Harvard and MIT and spread to Columbia, to Princeton, to Berkeley and elsewhere. This is a tried and true form of academic activism. It was used widely during the struggle against apartheid in South Africa during the 1970s and 1980s. We have to ask, Where is the anti-Semitism in criticizing Israel for its practices?

Summers set the tone for equating criticism of Israel with anti-Semitism. That was followed a few weeks later by an invitation to Tom Paulin, a Protestant from Northern Island who teaches at Oxford. He is one of the four or five most prominent poets in the United Kingdom today. He's also a very fine critic, whom I've published in the series I run at Harvard called "Convergences." He's a wonderful lecturer, and he appears often on BBC as a critic on a weekly program called "The Late Show," which deals with film, music, literature, and ballet. So he's an altogether extremely accomplished man, who had been invited to give the annual Morris Gray lecture in poetry at Harvard. A person who is not in the English Department and not a member of the faculty, Rita Goldberg, discovered that Paulin said in an interview that he detested Israeli settlers and that they reminded him of the SS. He had earlier written a poem about Mohammad Al-Dura, the young boy who was photographed in the arms of his father, who was shot and killed by Israeli soldiers. The boy became a kind of symbolic figure for the Intifada.

176   **Culture and Resistance**

Goldberg brought this to the attention of the faculty via a small committee, which then consulted with Summers. And Summers said that he believed in free speech and academic freedom, but that he would be disconcerted by the presence of Paulin on campus, and the invitation was rescinded. Of course, I was outraged, because what Tom said may have been intemperate and angry, but it certainly was a justified response to horrible outrages that are barely commented on in the media.

You notice, by the way, that almost every day in the *New York Times* there's an article about Israel and, at the very end, in the last paragraph, you read that "today, three more Palestinians were killed." We are killed like flies, and nobody says anything. What I think Tom Paulin was expressing was a kind of outrage at Israel's practices, which is his right. So he's immediately accused of anti-Semitism.

But then the English Department met again, and he has subsequently been reinvited. So all this goes to suggest that it's not just about free speech. It really is about the attempt to equate criticism of Israel with anti-Semitism, which is profoundly unjust, manipulative, and opportunistic. First of all, it suggests how terrified the supporters of Israel have become, by virtue of the fact that the whole world knows that Israel is flouting every known convention in its treatment of Palestinians. But also, for the first time I think, there's a sense in this country that Israel no longer enjoys the immunity from criticism that it had before. So they react by using their power, their influence, and scare tactics to make people feel that they are anti-Semites.

I would also add secondly that the situation on campuses has been further inflamed by the existence of a Web site which is designed specifically to report academics who criticize Israel or who seem to be proponents of the Palestinians.[17] It's led by someone named Daniel Pipes, who is basically a second-rate, unemployed scholar, who uses a further tactic, which is to associate criticism of Israel with anti-Americanism. So it's not just anti-Semitism, it's also anti-Americanism. And an outrageous Israeli, Martin Kramer, uses his Web site to attack everybody who says anything that he doesn't like. For example, he has described Columbia as "the Bir Zeit [university] on the Hudson," because there are two Palestinians teaching here.[18] Two Palestinians teaching in a faculty of 8,000 people! If you have two Palestinians, it makes you a kind of terrorist hideout. This is part of the atmosphere of intimidation that is McCarthyite.

Daniel Pipes is the director of something called the Middle East Forum, based in Philadelphia. He's a frequent talk-show guest. The situation abounds in ironies. One, of course, is that Arabs are Semites.

"Anti-Semitism" is never used to describe people who attack Arabs. I think we should make a practice of calling hate speech against Arabs "anti-Semitism." Historically, in nineteenth-century Europe, anti-Semitism included both Jews and Arabs.

178   **Culture and Resistance**

This gets onto delicate ground, because clearly there are people who hate Jews.

I think one has to acknowledge the existence of a horrific history of anti-Semitism—especially European and Christian anti-Semitism. In Europe, this anti-Semitism climaxed in the Holocaust. For anyone to deny the horrendous experience of anti-Semitism and the Holocaust is unacceptable. We don't want anybody's history of suffering to go unrecorded and unacknowledged. On the other hand, there's a great difference between acknowledging Jewish oppression and using that as a cover for the oppression of another people. One has to be able to distinguish between what happened to the Jews in World War II, and in Europe in the centuries of open and institutionalized anti-Semitism, and what people feel about the terrible practices of military occupation and dispossession in Palestine. Don't forget that what Israel does it does openly in the name of the Jewish people. It's not as if it's being done in the name of the Chinese people or some other group. So the association between Jew and Israel and Israeli practices is promoted by Israel itself.

I remember once on the West Bank when I was making a film, I saw some Israeli bulldozers tearing up some agricultural land belonging to Arabs. I asked the Israelis, "How could you do this? This land belongs to these people and they've been working on it for generations." He said, "It's not their land. It's the land of the people of Israel." So I said, "There you are, using this phrase 'the people of Israel' to oppress another people,

At the Rendezvous of Victory   **179**

and expecting everybody to go along with you simply because of Jewish suffering in Europe. You can't bring it here and use it as a cover for the dispossession another people."

I think anti-Semitism has to be very carefully adjudicated. Distinctions have to be made between anti-Semitism in the past in Europe, the emergence of new forms of anti-Semitism in countries such as Austria and France—which is genuinely anti-Semitic, in the sense that there's a hatred of Jews for the fact that they are Jews—and the kind of feelings about Israel that are now quite prevalent in the Middle East, which are really connected not to Jewishness as such, but to the practices of Israel as the state of the Jewish people. They have a different basis. European anti-Semitism is theological. It's based in Christian theology. There's a kind of distrust and opprobrium attached to Jews as the crucifiers of Christ. Catholicism has a long history, for example, of damning the Jews. That doesn't at all exist in Islam, where the Jews are considered "people of the book." It's true that in countries such as Saudi Arabia and Egypt there has been an attempt to import anti-Semitic tracts from Europe, such as *The Protocols of the Elders of Zion*. But that's fairly infrequent, and it has a very different basis than classical European anti-Semitism.

How can suffering be measured or compared?

It's scandalous and offensive to compare suffering. To say that "what they are doing to the Palestinians is what they did to the Jews" is not true at all. What the Jews went through is horrendous, and really without precedent. But on the other

180   **Culture and Resistance**

hand, that can't be used as a way of diminishing the terrible punishment that Palestinians have suffered at the hands of Israelis. It's not a matter of comparison. It's a matter of saying that both are unacceptable.

I'm particularly interested, as an Armenian, in this whole issue.

When I was in speaking at UCLA, an Armenian asked, "Do you associate the Armenian genocide with what happened to the Jews or with what has happened to the Palestinians?" I said why bother to compare them? They are all terrible historical experiences, in and of themselves. Obviously, there are common features. Lots of people have been killed and have suffered unnecessarily. There's a kind of underlying sense of cruelty which is common to them all. But they're all forms of suffering that are unacceptable and shouldn't be allowed to continue.

I remember June Jordan, the writer and poet who died in 2002, making the point about not quantifying suffering.

Yes. And not really comparing it, in the sense of quantifying it. What about African American suffering? One of the points I have made in recent lectures is that there has been a great deal of suffering in this country, which goes still unacknowledged. I am one of those who believes that there never is a term or time period for suffering. In other words, you can't say suffering begins here and ends there. It goes on. It's written into the experiences of people—of the Armenians, of the Jews, of the Palestinians—and nobody's in a position to

At the Rendezvous of Victory

say, "Well, you've talked enough about suffering. Let's move on to something else." Many people are now saying things like this about slavery, about the Holocaust, about the Armenian genocide. There's no calendar for when something begins and when something ends. The distortions that are imposed upon the lives of people, even several generations after the actual suffering, continue for a long time. It's very difficult to assign them a beginning, a middle, and an end.

In 1915, Armenians were the victims of the first genocide of the twentieth century, at the hands of the Turks. Stephen Kinzer wrote an article a few years ago entitled "Armenia Never Forgets. Maybe It Should."[9] The general tenor of the piece was "get over it." This generated literally no response, no comment. Imagine if Kinzer had suggested that the Jews forget their past.

I had an experience once that was rather similar. It was in 1988. There was a *Tikkun* conference in New York, organized by Michael Lerner. I, and my friend Ibrahim Abu-Lughod were on a panel with Michael Walzer. At one point, in a moment of exasperation, Walzer said, "All right, you're going to get your state, so I think it's important to stop thinking about the past. You go have your state, we'll have ours, and that's the end of it." At which point, a woman in the audience, who I'll never forget—her name was Hilda Silverstein—got up in a state of rage, railing at Walzer, saying, "How dare you tell a Palestinian that he should stop reminding us of the past, when you and I belong to a people that is always reminding the world of how much we suffered, and asking people never to forget?

182   **Culture and Resistance**

How dare you tell a Palestinian to forget?" When we remember and when we forget is something for ourselves to decide, and not for people to tell us. I think it's an obscenity for Jews today, whether they're Israelis or Americans, to tell Palestinians, "Stop turning yourselves into victims. Start blaming yourselves." Unfortunately, there's a significant number of Arab intellectuals who take the same tone, and say "Let's stop talking about the evils of imperialism and Zionism. Let's start talking about our self-inflicted wounds." People like Fouad Ajami and Kanan Makiya. It's a profound self-abjection, which I deeply resent. It suits perfectly the neoconservative idea that people are responsible for their own disasters. As if imperialism never happened, as if genocide never happened, as if ethnic cleansing never happened. I just think it's outrageous.

The Czech writer Milan Kundera, in his book, The Book of Laughter and Forgetting *writes, "the struggle of man against power is the struggle of memory against forgetting."*[20]

The lectures I give now always feature the importance of memory to the Palestinian experience. Not organized memory, because we don't have a state and we don't have an organized, central authority. But if you look in every Palestinian household, into the third generation after 1948, you'll find such objects as house keys, letters, titles, deeds, photographs, newspaper clippings, kept to preserve the memory of a period when our existence was relatively whole. Memory is a powerful collective instrument for preserving identity. And it's something that can be carried not only through official narra-

At the Rendezvous of Victory

tives and books, but also through informal memory. It is one of the main bulwarks against historical erasure. It is a means of resistance.

The inflections of Palestinian colloquial speech are preserved into the third and fourth generation. My son, for example, who grew up in New York, subsequently learned Arabic. When you hear him speak, you can hear the accents of his grandfather. He obviously heard it from me and he heard it from other Palestinians when we speak together. So speech itself is really a great tablet of memory, which has to be activated and used. But it does carry forward the past into the present and into the future, and keeps it from disappearing, going down the memory hole.

You often mine literature to demonstrate this very point about memory. Borges wrote a story that you've discussed, "Funes, His Memory."[21] Another story that you've refered to is "In the Penal Colony," by Kafka.[22]

There I was trying to describe something which is not at all appreciated in the United States or even in Western Europe. I was talking about Kafka in order to illustrate the detailed level of oppression of Palestinians by Israelis. How do you design an apparatus to break the collective will, to destroy the wish to live, from morning until night? This is what Kafka was exploring. Every step of Palestinian life, from going to school or to work or to the market, is regulated by the Israeli military. You have to go through checkpoints. If you want to go to the hospital, in the case of emergency, you still have to stand in line for hours. People have died that way. Schools are rou-

184   **Culture and Resistance**

tinely closed. There are hundreds of checkpoints on the West Bank alone. Gaza is a gigantic prison, enclosed entirely on three sides—the fourth side being the sea—by an electrical fence. Bombing, the demolition of houses, the destruction of agricultural fields, the building of this fence, which separates villagers from their lands, the detention of young men, are all ways of humiliating and punishing Palestinians.

In this story, Kafka shows how the invention of a fantastic torture machine—which is so detailed in its infliction of pain by needles that inscribe writing upon the human body—in the end, captures the user and inventor of the machine himself. I think the same thing is happening with the Israelis. The Israeli military is used to humiliating and subjugating the Palestinians, but it may be hurting the Israelis more than it hurts the Palestinians, who have triumphed in acts of heroism of just survival against all these obstacles placed in their way.

You just mentioned the memory hole, and that of course brings up George Orwell. In Reflections on Exile, *you have an essay on Orwell, entitled "Tourism Among the Dogs."*[23]

I think Orwell is a complicated case of a man who was a very gifted observer, who was drawn to situations of extreme suffering, as in the case of the miners he writes about in *The Road to Wigan Pier,* for example.[24] He was one of the first to write in a detailed way about human cruelty under imperialism. But he was also a man who remained detached from the objects he was describing. There's no known record, except in *Homage to Catalonia,* of Orwell being part of any movement.[25]

At the Rendezvous of Victory

His later years were marked by paranoia and a kind of misanthropic sense of the people around him, some of whom he thought of as "pansies" and "Reds." His writing contains an extraordinarily unattractive combination of a fierce sense of injustice and a dislike of people. Orwell was also deeply Anglophilic. For him, the center of the world was England. He had no great love for Indians or Blacks or Jews. In fact, he was anti-Semitic, and, as it turns out, also quite anti-Zionist.

England was the center of his world, but he also was critical about the workings of empire. He wrote about his experiences in Burma, where he was serving as a policeman and was witness to a hanging.[26]

Yes, he exposed injustice, but to me in only a very limited way. I don't think one feels, reading Orwell, that he's moved by a will to emancipation or liberation. It's more about exposing and attacking than about opening people to new resources of hope. He is one of these writers who simply was never in touch with a grassroots movement, and never felt himself to be part of a general cause. There's a sense of isolation and even of misanthropic hostility toward the other. And it's wonderfully manifest in *1984*, where everybody is a potential enemy.[27]

That novel, his last work, which came out in 1949, is being mentioned today because of the Bush administration's attack on civil liberties and its announcement of an era of permanent war.

I think he was right that this is the state that we're moving toward. But I think he doesn't present an alternative to that. The Orwellian vision is a bleak and limited one. I don't think

186 **Culture and Resistance**

he's in touch with hope, with liberation, with critical engagement, with association or affiliation between people. The idea of human progress is quite outside his vision.

You mentioned Homage to Catalonia, *his reportage from the Spanish Civil War. That reminded me of the bombing of the Basque town Guernica by the German air force in 1937. At the entrance to the United Nations, there had been a reproduction of the famous painting "Guernica," by Picasso. Ironically, that has been covered over. Apparently, the depiction of war and decapitated heads and flying limbs was simply too much for people who are now discussing the destruction of Iraq.*

The painting's cover-up was done initially in honor of Colin Powell's visit to address the Security Council. There's a widespread feeling that any reminder of the kind of damage and horror that war might cause ought to be removed. Everything should be sanitized and turned into CNN-style coverage, where war has become an electronic rather than a human experience. What you see are exultant and triumphalist weapons that make the horrors of war a very distant thing. I think it's a way of accommodating people to the idea of war as something that we can engage in without much damage to ourselves or to others.

And if it happens to others, it's "collateral damage."

And you don't even have to see it.

In Arabic, the word for storyteller is hakawati. *You are the* hakawati *in the United States, in terms of telling the Palestinian story.*

At the Rendezvous of Victory

Over the years, I've seen you introduce new combinations of notes, new chord structures, new permutations to advance the piece, to tell the story, as it were.

What is amazing to me is the persistence of the Palestinian story, and the many different turns it takes, and the fact that it isn't an organized story, because we are a stateless and exiled people. One has to keep telling the story in as many ways as possible, as insistently as possible, and in as compelling a way as possible, to keep attention to it, because there is always a fear that it might just disappear.

I think one of the roles of the intellectual at this point is to provide a counterpoint, by storytelling, by reminders of the graphic nature of suffering, and by reminding everyone that we're talking about people. We're not talking about abstractions.

In late January 2003, Columbia University hosted a Palestinian film festival called "Dreams of a Nation." One of the films was Divine Intervention, *by Elia Suleiman, who* The Nation *calls "one of the most extraordinary writer/ actor/ directors in contemporary film."[28] Can film be used as a tool, as a method to advance a political cause?*

Absolutely. The festival was organized by an Iranian colleague of mine, Hamid Dabashi, in the Middle East Languages Department. There were about seventy films shown. And what is especially impressive is that every one of the sessions was full. They were oversubscribed. There were hordes of people who couldn't get in.

188　　　　　　　**Culture and Resistance**

The thing about Elia Suleiman's film that was so unusual, and justifiably drew attention to itself, was that it's not, in the strict sense of the word, a militant, propagandistic film. On the contrary, it's a very understated, satirical film, very much in the style of Buster Keaton or Jacques Tati. It includes long periods of silence and sight gags involving Israeli troops and Palestinians. In the film, the experience of occupation is depicted with humor, not as suffering in the classical sense of the word. I think what attracted attention to the film is its studied casualness.

Divine Intervention *was submitted to the Academy for an Oscar nomination. What happened to it?*

It was entered in the category of foreign film, but the Motion Picture Academy refused it, saying there's no country called Palestine.[29] Therefore, you can't enter the film. But this is typical. It goes back to the Mahmoud Darwish poem about the identity card. Many Palestinian identity cards don't list "Palestinian" as one's nationality; they list one's nationality as "undetermined." That is the status of the Palestinians today. Everyone knows that Palestine exists, but some refuse to acknowledge it, except as "undetermined."

In the media today, you see an open embrace for imperialism, for war, and the projection and celebration of American power.

People like Michael Ignatieff, Max Boot, and George Will are elaborators of other people's thoughts. They are the apologists of empire. They are not the makers of imperial opinion. They consolidate opinion. They elaborate it. They give it a kind of intellectual cover. But none of them is an original thinker. They are products of the system, and are used by the system to provide cover for the acts of naked aggression that have taken place in the name of American values. But as Joseph Conrad said, "The conquest of the earth … is not a pretty thing when you look into it too much." It involves taking land away from people who have "flatter noses" and darker skins than ourselves.[30]

That rationale for imperialism in Conrad's time was the White Man's Burden, a mission civilizatrice. *Today it's the "war on terrorism."*

The "war on terrorism" and the "fight for democracy," as it's called. Bush says we're going to fight for good against evil, and that we're going to spread democratic values, American values, all over the world. Every empire does two things: It begins by saying it's not like any of the empires of the past, and second, it always talks not in terms of destruction, but in fact of the opposite. That it's bringing enlightenment and civilization, peace and progress to the other people. The apologists for empire never say it openly, but to them the conquered are lesser people. Therefore, we have to bring all these wonderful things to them. It was true in Conrad's day one hundred years ago, and it's true today.

What has emboldened the imperialists today?

One reason is the absence of a powerfully organized and consistently mobilized counterforce. I don't think it's enough

190   **Culture and Resistance**

to say that it's because of the demise of the Soviet Union. I think it's also a failure of the intellectual class, with a few exceptions here and there. There's so much factionalism, so much sectarianism, so much petty squabbling over definitions and identities that people have lost sight of the important goal, as Aimé Césaire described it, the rendezvous of victory, where all peoples in search of freedom and emancipation and enlightenment gather. One of the reasons for this failure has been what is called postmodernism, in which American pragmatism and linguistic analysis as well as French deconstructionism have played a very important role. The intellectual class has simply turned away from the great narratives of enlightenment and emancipation. Jean Baudrillard tells us that those days are over.

Another critical reason is the failure of representative democracy. In a two-party system like ours—and in England—the other party simply becomes part of the game, and not part of the opposition. The idea of opposition has disappeared from the scene of formal politics. Now it is lodged elsewhere—in the university, in the church, in the labor movement, and so on. I think it's a collective struggle. I don't think by any means it's something to be done by star intellectuals or people from the top. Quite the contrary.

Thomas Friedman said a very interesting thing on The Charlie Rose Show *on February 13. He said that Iraq is "a country that very few Americans know anything about."[31] Rose simply said nothing, and went on to his next question. I thought that was very revealing.*

I think it's even more revealing that Friedman didn't press the point that the United States is mobilizing for war against a country about which we know virtually nothing.

Let me see if I can bring in some musical analogies here, because music is so much a part of who you are. Have the corporate media, and perhaps the educational system, rendered many Americans tone deaf, unable to distinguish the different notes?

Yes, people's analytical powers are dulled and anesthetized. And the result is that you get an immediate acceptance of what is easy. You forget about all the complexities and difficulties.

Plutarch once said that to create harmony in music, one must investigate discord.

Adorno suggests that music is really best understood through dissonance, not through consonance. I think there's something to that. What makes music interesting is the balance between dissonance and consonance, with the weight of a piece really based in dissonance and discord, rather than the other way around.

I know you don't like to talk about yourself, but I want to ask, being Edward W. Said, what kind of a burden is that? You know that you're being watched, you know that your every move, your every utterance is being monitored. Do you get tired of it? Do you wish you could just play the piano or watch a good tennis match?

192   **Culture and Resistance**

Rarely. I usually feel too busy and harried to think much about it. Many years ago, I learned not to be too self-conscious about what others think of me. I think I have enough to do trying to get through the day, especially since I have been ill. I've been in treatment now for nine years. I spend a tremendous amount of energy trying to keep going, in spite of weakness and many, many crises. So you tend to focus on what's important, and how you're viewed by others is not really very high on my list.

In your memoir, Out of Place, *you write, "I occasionally experience myself as a cluster of flowing currents.... [w]ith so many dissonances in my life."*[32]

I don't think of myself as a coherent, single person. I'm many different things. And I don't try to balance between them. I don't see myself as somebody who's trying to patch up all the differences. I try to live in the differences.

In the many times we have talked, when I ask about your health, you always say, "I've got to press on."

Very much so. A lot of that is due to my doctor. I should have probably died four or five years ago. But he's an ingenious man, a wonderful physician, and a great scientist. His ingenuity in dealing with this insidious and cruel disease has inspired me to keep fighting. Which is what I do. And I enjoy life, I must say. I'm surrounded by people I love. I love teaching. I get a tremendous energy out of the students I interact with—not as much as I would like to these days, because my teaching is curtailed. But being a member of an academic community, and a wider political community of activists and people who feel they are moving toward liberation and understanding is very exhilarating. In fact, I can't think of anything better I'd like to be doing.

Notes

1   Michael Jansen, "Military Is Deliberately Destroying State Structures Built by Palestinians," *Irish Times,* April 16, 2002, p. 9.

2   Jansen, "Military Is Deliberately Destroying," p. 9. See also Justin Huggler and Phil Reeves, "What Really Happened When Israeli Forces Went Into Jenin?" *The Independent* (London), April 25, 2002, pp. 4–7.

3   Mahmoud Darwish, "Identity Card," in *Splinters of Bone*, trans. B.M. Benani (New York: Greenfield Review Press, 1974), pp. 13–14.

4   Mahmoud Darwish, "A State of Siege," available online at http://www.mafhoum.com/press3/92C10.htm.

5   Pablo Neruda, "Explica Algunas Cosas/I'm Explaining a Few Things," in *Selected Poems*, ed. Nathaniel Tarn (New York: Delta, 1972), pp. 150–55.

6   Tim Rutten, "The Poets Fly Like Doves," *Los Angeles Times,* September 12, 2003, p. 5: 2.

7   Seattle Times News Service, "Impact of Old DUI Unclear as GOP Charges Dirty Trick," *Seattle Times,* November 4, 2001, p. A1.

8   Peter Ford, "Antiwar Movement Awakens over Iraq," *Christian Science Monitor,* February 18, 2003, p. 1; Anastasia Hendrix, Pamela J. Podger, and Steve Rubenstein, "Peaceful S.F. Crowd Protests Stance on Iraq," *San Francisco Chronicle,* February 17, 2003, p. A1.

9   Angelique Chrisafis et al., "Millions Worldwide Rally for Peace," *The Guardian* (London), February 17, 2003, p. 6; Todd Richissin, "Millions March for Peace," *Baltimore Sun,* February 16, 2003, p. 1A.

194   **Culture and Resistance**

10   David Barsamian, *The Decline and Fall of Public Broadcasting* (Cambridge: South End Press, 2001).

11   "Size of protest—it's like deciding, well, I'm going to decide policy based upon a focus group," Bush said. "The role of a leader is to decide policy based upon the security, in this case, the security of the people." Quoted in Richard W. Stevenson, "Antiwar Protests Fail to Sway Bush on Plans for Iraq," *New York Times*, February 19, 2003, p. A1.

12   David E. Sanger, "Bush Tells Critics Hussein Could Strike at Any Time," *New York Times,* October 6, 2002, p. 1: 22.

13   Dan Plesch, "Operation Regime Change," *The Guardian* (London), February 19, 2003, p. 17.

14   James Bennet, "Palestinian Subdued and Shot, Yet His Bomb Kills Three," *New York Times,* October 28, 2002, p. A3.

15   Justin Brown, "Saddam's Rise Puts Pressure on US Officials," *Christian Science Monitor,* September 21, 2000, p. 1.

16   Claire Sanders, "Harvard Drops Paulin's Talk," *Times Higher Education Supplement,* November 15, 2002, p. 52. See also Claire Sanders, "Harvard Makes U-turn and Asks Paulin Back," *Times Higher Education Supplement,* November 22, 2002, p. 48.

17   See Tanya Schevitz, "Professors Want Own Names Put on Mideast Blacklist," *San Francisco Chronicle,* September 28, 2002, p. A2.

18   Martin Kramer, "The Columbia Club of Middle Eastern Studies," http://www.MartinKramer.org, November 5, 2002.

19   Stephen Kinzer, "Armenia Never Forgets. Maybe It Should," *New York Times,* October 4, 1998, p. 4: 16.

20   Milan Kundera, *The Book of Laughter and Forgetting,* trans. Aaron Asher (New York: HarperPerennial, 1999), p. 3.

21   Jorge Luis Borges, "Funes, His Memory," in *Collected Fictions,* trans. Andrew Hurley (New York: Penguin, 1999), pp. 131–37. See also "Unresolved Geographies, Embattled Landscapes," lecture by Edward W. Said, Hampshire College, Amherst, MA, September 17, 1999. Text available from Alternative Radio.

At the Rendezvous of Victory   195

22 Franz Kafka, "In The Penal Colony," in *The Complete Stories* (New York: Schocken, 1995), pp. 140–67. See also Edward W. Said, "Punishment by Detail," *Al-Ahram Weekly*, August 8–14, 2002.

23 Edward W. Said, "Tourism Among the Dogs," in *Reflections on Exile and Other Essays* (Cambridge: Harvard University Press, 2002), pp. 93–97.

24 George Orwell, *The Road to Wigan Pier* (New York: Harvest Books, 1973).

25 George Orwell, *Homage to Catalonia* (New York: Harvest Books, 1987).

26 George Orwell, "A Hanging," in *Essays*, ed. John Carey (New York: Knopf/Everyman's Library, 1996), pp. 16–20.

27 George Orwell, *1984* (New York: Knopf, 1992).

28 Divine Intervention, dir. Elia Suleiman (New York: Avatar Films, 2002).

29 Stuart Klawans. "The Eastern Front: Films of the Present Conflict," *Nation*, February 10, 2003, p. 34.

30 Joseph Conrad, *Heart of Darkness* (New York: Penguin, 1999), p. 31.

31 Thomas Friedman, "Thomas Friedman on Iraq and the UN," interview by Charlie Rose, PBS, *The Charlie Rose Show*, February 13, 2003. Online at http://www.charlierose.com/archives/archive.shtm.

32 Edward W. Said, *Out of Place: A Memoir* (New York: Vintage Books, 2000), p. 295.

Palestine Under the British Mandate

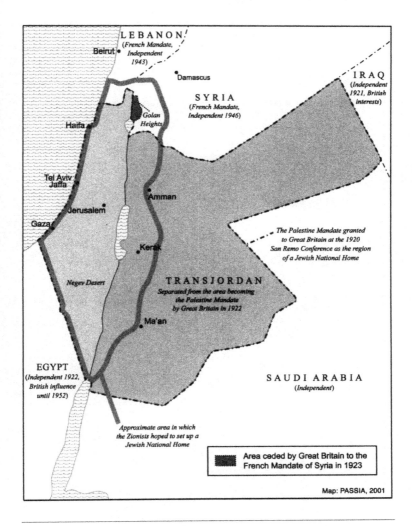

Maps source: Palestinian Academic Society for the Study of International Affairs (PASSIA), *The Palestine Question in Maps: 1878–2000* (Jerusalem: PASSIA, 2002). Maps also available online at http://www.passia.org.

Land Ownership in Palestine and the UN Partition Plan, 1947

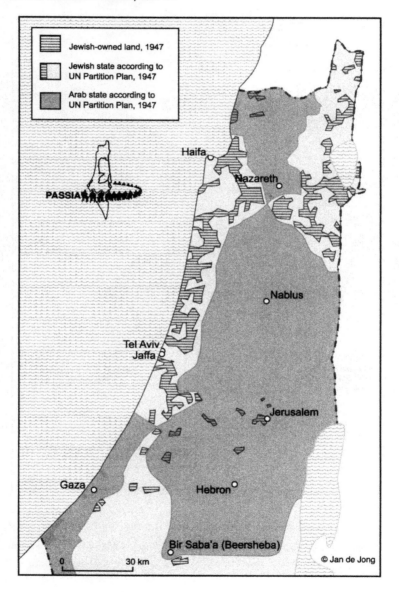

Palestinian Villages Depopulated in 1948 and Razed by Israel

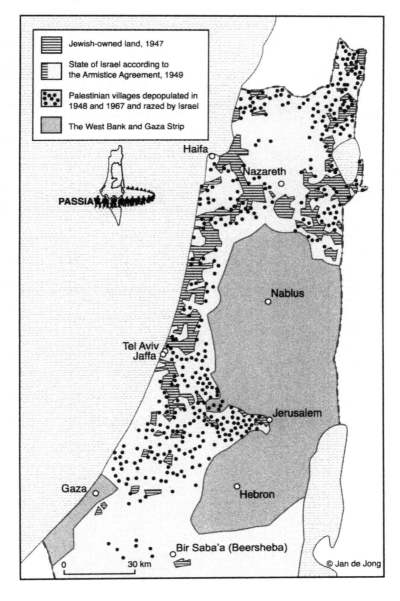

Interim (Oslo II) Agreement, September 28, 1995, TABA

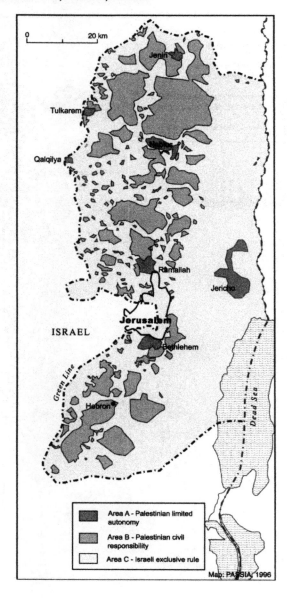

Maps 201

Wye River Memorandum, October 23, 1998

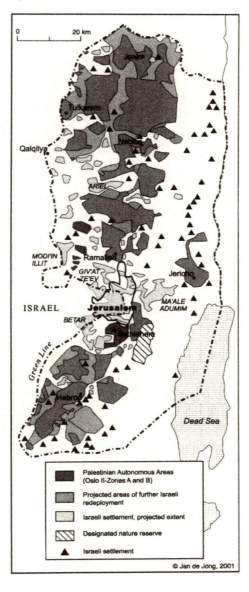

Sharm Esh-Sheikh Agreement, September 4, 1999

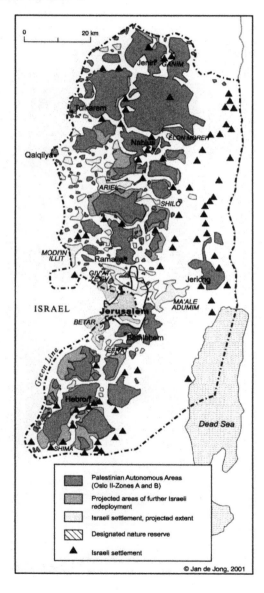

Camp David Projection, July 2000

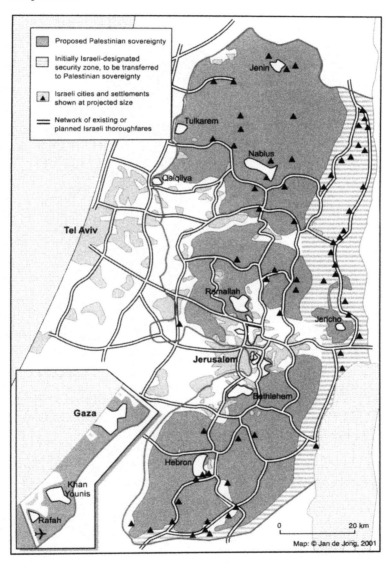

TABA Talks Projection, January 2001

TABA Talks Projection, January 2001 (continued)

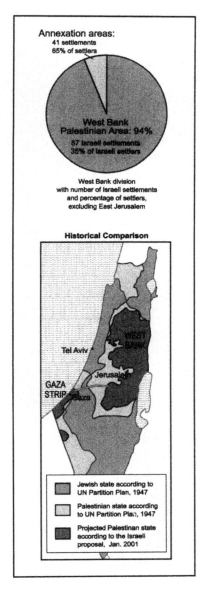

The Sharon Proposal, Spring 2001

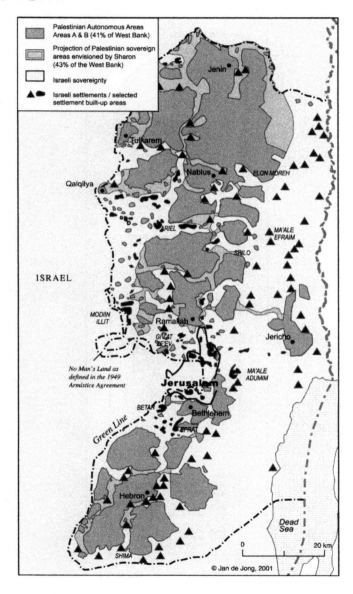

The Sharon Proposal, Spring 2001 (continued)

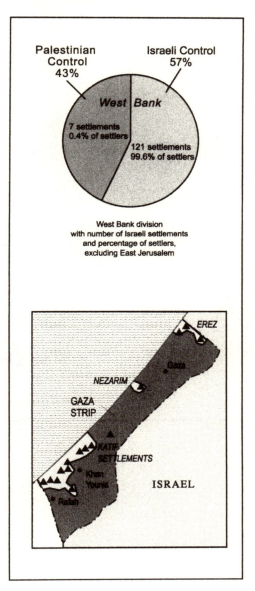

Municipal Boundaries of Jerusalem, 1947–2000

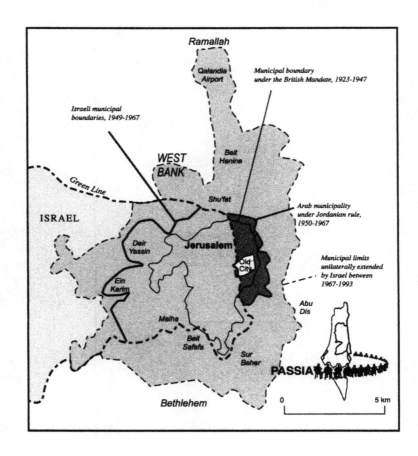

Maps 209

Projection of the Israeli Proposal for Jerusalem's Final Status at Camp David, July 2000

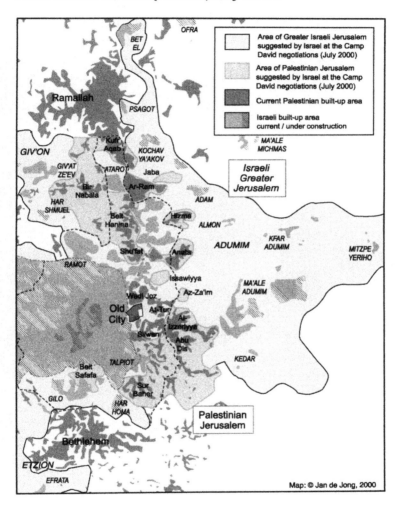

Map: © Jan de Jong, 2000

Edward W. Said Selected Bibliography

Parallels and Paradoxes: Explorations in Music and Society. With Daniel Barenboim. New York: Pantheon Books, 2002.

Reflections on Exile and Other Essays. Cambridge: Harvard University Press, 2002.

Power, Politics, and Culture: Interviews with Edward W. Said. Edited by Gauri Viswanathan. New York: Vintage Books, 2002.

The End of the Peace Process: Oslo and After. New York: Knopf, 2001.

"The Cruelty of Memory." *New York Review of Books* (November 30, 2000) 47 (19): 46–50.

The Edward Said Reader. Edited by Moustafa Bayoumi and Andrew Rubin. New York: Vintage Books, 2000.

The End of the Peace Process: Oslo and After. New York: Pantheon Books; London: Granta, 2000.

"Palestinians Under Seige." *London Review of Books* (December 14, 2000) 22 (24): 9–10, 12–14.

"Edward W. Said." Interview by David Barsamian. *The Progressive* (April 1999) 63 (4): 34–38.

212   **Culture and Resistance**

"Eqbal Ahmad, 1933–99." *The Nation* (May 31, 1999) 268 (20): 6–7.

"Leaving Palestine." *New York Review of Books* (September 23, 1999) 46 (14): 35–38.

"The One-State Solution." *New York Times Magazine* (January 10, 1999): 36–39.

Out of Place: A Memoir. New York: Knopf, 1999.

Covering Islam: How the Media and the Experts Determine How We See the Rest of the World. Updated and revised edition. New York: Vintage, 1997.

"The Real Meaning of the Hebron Agreement." *Journal of Palestine Studies* (Spring 1997) 26 (3): 31–36.

"An Intifada Against Betrayal, Despair." *Los Angeles Times* (October 2, 1996): B9.

"Lost Between War and Peace: In Arafat's Palestine." *London Review of Books* (September 5, 1996) 18 (17): 10–15.

Peace and Its Discontents: Essays on Palestine in the Middle East Peace Process. New York: Vintage, 1995.

"On Mahmoud Darwish." *Grand Street* (Winter 1994) 12 (4): 112–115.

The Pen and the Sword: Conversations with David Barsamian. Monroe, Maine: Common Courage Press, 1994.

Selected Bibliography 213

The Politics of Dispossession: The Struggle for Palestinian Self-Determination, 1969–1994. New York: Pantheon Books, 1994.

Representations of the Intellectual: The 1993 Reith Lectures. New York: Pantheon Books, 1994.

"Second Thoughts on Arafat's Deal." *Harper's Magazine* (January 1994) 288 (1724): 15–18.

"A Palestinian Versailles." *Progressive* (December 1993) 57 (12): 22–26.

Musical Elaborations. The Wellek Library Lectures at the University of California, Irvine. New York: Columbia University Press, 1991.

"C.L.R. James: A Life Beyond the Boundaries." *Washington Post* (March 5, 1989).

Blaming the Victims: Spurious Scholarship and the Palestinian Question. Edited with Christopher Hitchens. London: Verso, 1988.

After the Last Sky: Palestinian Lives. Photographs by Jean Mohr. New York: Pantheon; London: Faber, 1986.

"Orientalism Reconsidered." *Cultural Critique* (Fall 1985) 1: 89–107.

A Profile of the Palestinian People. With Ibrahim Abu-Lughod, Janet L. Abu-Lughod, Muhammad Hallaj, and

Elia Zureik. Chicago: Palestine Human Rights Campaign, 1983.

The World, the Text, and the Critic. Cambridge: Harvard University Press, 1983.

Orientalism. New York: Pantheon Books; London: Routledge & Kegan Paul; Toronto: Random House, 1978.

"The Arab Portrayed." In Ibrahim Abu-Lughod, ed., *The Arab-Israeli Confrontation of June 1967: An Arab Perspective*, pp. 1–9. Evanston, Ill.: Northwestern University Press, 1970.

"The Palestinian Experience." In Herbert Mason, ed., *Reflections on the Middle East Crisis,* pp. 127–147. Studies in the Behavioral Sciences, 7. The Hague & Paris: Mouton, 1970.

Beginnings: Intention and Method. New York: Basic Books, 1975. Paperback edition, Columbia University Press, 1987.

Joseph Conrad and the Fiction of Autobiography. Cambridge: Harvard University Press; London: Oxford University Press, 1966.

Index

A

Abbasid caliphate, 172
Abu-Lughod, Ibrahim, 181
activism. *See* movement building
Adonis, 161, 164
Adorno, Theodore, 164, 191
Afghanistan: Arabs and, 122;
    British contact with, 104; drug
    trade with Pakistan, 128;
    information on, 129; Soviet
    invasion of, 107, 111; U.S.
    bombing of, 118–19, 140–41
African Americans, 95, 180
Ahmad, Eqbal, 112, 114, 129,
    146–47, 153
Al-Ahram Weekly, 55
Ajami, Fouad, 125–26, 182
Albanians, 93
Albuquerque Journal, 73
Algeria: French colonialism in, 34,
    40, 89, 114, 161; Islamic
    fundamentalism in, 62
Alternative Radio, 58
American Jewish Committee, 74
"American Zionism" (Said), 55–56
Amnesty International, 88, 173
anti-Americanism: among Arabs,
    104–8; anti-Semitism associated

with, 177; cause of, 144, 153,
    168–69; ignorance of within
    U.S., 92
anti-Semitism: accusations of, 56,
    58, 74, 146–47, 175–77; by
    Christians, 152, 178–79; in
    Holocaust, 38, 44, 147–49,
    178–81; by Orwell, 185. *See also*
    racism
Al-Aqsa Intifada: as
    anti-colonialist, 36–38, 71–72;
    binational state and, 63;
    casualty rates, 66n5, 72–73;
    causes of, 33–34, 40–43; Israeli
    Palestinian support for, 49–50;
    media on, 58; results of, 71–73
Arabic, 3, 21, 161, 164–65, 183
Arab League, 77
"Arab Portrayed, The" (Said), ix
Arabs: anti-Americanism among,
    104–8, 144; anti-Semitism
    against, 177; Arabic language, 3,
    21, 161, 164–65, 183; and
    democracy, 58–59, 169;
    diversity among, 146;
    geopolitical strategy and, 93; in
    Hebron, 54–55; information
    on, 129; intellectuals, 154, 182;

216   **Culture and Resistance**

Iraq as cultural center of, 171–72; Israel, 47–48; parochialism of, 15–20; refugees and, 96; social movements and, 153–54; stereotypes of, 53, 74, 82–83, 122–24, 165–66; "street" and, 170; tolerance of Jews by, 148; in U.S., 59–60, 78, 82–83, 145; unity among, 62; visiting Palestine, 16–18. *See also specific countries*

Arafat, Suha, 15

Arafat, Yasir: control by, 1–2; control of, 39, 40, 76; criticism of, x, 7, 81; health of, 1; Intifada and, 37; media demonization of, 110; as negotiator, 33, 43–45, 81, 136–37

Arendt, Hannah, 7–9

"Armenia Never Forgets" (Kinzer), 181

Armenians, 94, 171, 180–81

arms: Israel's superiority, 34, 48; supplied by U.S., 60–61, 75, 105, 111, 139, 150–51

Aronson, Geoffrey, 39

assassination, 25, 76, 126, 138, 156n11

Assyrians, 171

Austria, 14, 85–87, 179

B

B'Tselem, 173

Balfour Declaration, 53

Barak, Ehud: assassination by, 25; in the peace process, 43, 45–46; settlement increase under, 55, 75; Sharon's Al-Aqsa visit and, 41, 42

Barenboim, Daniel, 23–26, 65

Baudrillard, Jean, 190

BBC, 57

Begin, Menachem, 147

Beilin, Yossi, 45–46

Beit Hanina, 5

Bellingham, Washington, 80

Ben & Jerry's ice cream, 77

Ben-Gurion, David, 8, 9, 147

Berger, Sandy, 124

binational state, 5–7, 63–64, 148–49

bin Laden, Osama: motivation of, 115–16; mythologizing of, 109; presaging of, 153; terrorism and, 90, 119; U.S. targeting of, 140, 141; U.S. support for, 107, 110–11

Bir Zeit, 24

Bishara, Azmi, 6, 10–11

Black, Conrad, 82, 84

Blair, Tony, 117

Boeing, 150

Book of Laughter and Forgetting, The (Kundera), 182

Boot, Max, 188

Borges, Jorge Luis, 183

Britain. *See* United Kingdom

Buber, Martin, 7, 9

Burns, John, 83

Bush, George: ignorance of, 135; Iraq war and, 167, 169, 171, 172, 194n11; metaphysics and, 141, 143–44, 189; September 11 and, 109; support for, 152, 153; unilateralism of, 121

Bush, Laura, 166

Bush administration, 76, 185

C

Caterpillar, 136, 151

Index   **217**

censorship, 2–4, 57–58, 84–87
Césaire, Aimé, xi, 190
Chaldeans, 171
Charlie Rose Show, 4, 124–25, 140, 190–91
Cheney, Dick, 167
China, 37
Chomsky, Noam, 40, 80, 84–85
Christianity, 148, 151–52, 171, 178–79
Clark, Wesley, 124
Clinton, Bill, 7, 89
Clinton, Hillary, 91, 145
Clinton administration, 72, 146
Cockburn, Alexander, 40
collectivism vs. individuality, 98–99
colonialism: 34, 40, 89, 174; by British in Israel, 9, 35, 147, 148; by British in other countries, 34, 40, 89; by French in Algeria, 34, 40, 89, 114, 161; by Israel against Palestinians, 34, 36–38, 71–72, 97; in the U.S., 78, 97
Columbia University, 124, 173, 177, 187
Commentary, 61, 82
Commission of Inquiry into the Events at the Refugee Camps in Beirut, 41
communism, 107
Conrad, Joseph, 189
Constant, Emmanuel, 120
Covering Islam (Said), 124
culture: art, 186; films, 57–58, 122, 187–88; Iraq and, 171–72; literature, 184–87; music, xi, 23–26, 65, 191; poetry, xi, 161–64, 166–67, 175–76; resistance and, 159–61
Culture and Imperialism (Said), xi, 3

Culture, Politics, and Power (Said), 65
curfews, 133, 136

D

Dabashi, Hamid, 187
Darwish, Mahmoud, xi, 161–63, 188
Dayan, Moshe, 22
defense, 34, 136–39
democracy: in Arab countries, 58–59, 169; failure of, 169, 190; U.S. lack of, 105–6, 144, 168, 189
demographics, 7, 48
Des Moines Register, 88
detainment, 138, 141
displacement: in 1948, 31–32, 147; colonialism and, 174; illegality of, 138; mythology and, 21–23, 178–79; Oslo talks and, 96; resistance to, 18, 63, 71–72. *See also* al-Nakba; refugees
divestment movement, 151, 173, 175
Divine Intervention, 187–88
drug trade, 128
Al-Dura, Mohammed, 175

E

East Jerusalem, 32, 42, 133
Eban, Abba, 45
economics: globalization, 61, 90, 99; suffering and, 73, 77, 116–17, 127. *See also* foreign aid
Economist, 36
Egypt: anti-Semitism in, 179; arms and employment in, 150–51; culture in, 3, 15, 153, 172; emigrants from, 78; Gaza ruled

218   **Culture and Resistance**

by, 50; information on, 129; Islam and, 62, 126–27; location of, 48; normalization with Israel, 16, 47; regional role of, 91, 93; social movements in, 59, 153; U.S. imperialism and, 142–43

Emerson, Steven, 89, 90

employment, 2, 5, 77, 136–37, 150–51

England. *See* United Kingdom

F

Faiz, Faiz Ahmed, 161–62

films, 57–58, 122, 187–88

Finkelstein, Norman, 95

Fisk, Robert, 40, 87

Fo, Dario, 116

Ford Foundation, 18

foreign aid (from U.S. to Israel), 35, 60, 74–75, 105, 135–36

Foundation for Middle East Peace, 39

France: Algeria and, 34, 40, 89, 114, 161; anti-Semitism in, 179; terrorism by, 113

Freud, Sigmund, 86

Freud Museum Institute (London), 86–87

Freud Society of Vienna, 85–87

Friedman, Thomas, 43, 84, 190–91

"Funes, His Memory" (Borges), 183

G

Gemayal, Bashir, 143

generational shifts, 6, 12–13, 79

Geneva Convention, 138, 169

Germany, 26, 53, 77, 148. *See also* Holocaust

Gilmour, Ian, 84

Giuliani, Rudolph, 109

globalization, 61, 90, 99

Goldberg, Rita, 175–76

Goldstein, Baruch, 54

Great Britain. *See* United Kingdom

Guantánamo Bay, 141

"Guernica" (Picasso), 186

H

Ha'aretz, 56–57, 85

Haider, Jörg, 86

Haiti, 120

hakawati, 186–87

Halberstam, David, 125

Hamas, 61–62, 138

Hartford Courant, 88

Harvard University, 174–76

Heaney, Seamus, 162

Heart of Darkness (Conrad), 115

Hebron, 5, 54–55

Herzl, Theodor, 53

hijackings, 114

history. *See* memory; storytelling

Hitchens, Christopher, 145

Hitler, Adolf, 73

Hitti, Philip, 129

Hoagland, Jim, 125

Holocaust: anti-Semitism and, 38, 44, 147–49, 178–81; culture and, 26; Freud and, 86; other suffering and, 38, 44, 73, 94–95, 147–49, 178–81

Holocaust Industry (Finkelstein), 95

Homage to Catalonia (Orwell), 184, 186

Hourani, Albert, 129

Human Rights Watch, 88, 173

hunger, 133–35

Index

219

Huntington, Samuel, 89
Hussein, Saddam, 91, 110–11, 172

I

"I'm Explaining a Few Things"
    (Neruda), 163
"Identity Card" (Darwish), 161
Ignatieff, Michael, 145, 188
immigration laws, 96–97
imperialism: Orwell on, 184; by the
    U.S., 59, 88–91, 104–7, 140–44,
    167–69, 188–91; "war on
    terrorism" and, 88–91, 140–44,
    189. *See also* colonialism
individuality vs. collectivism, 98–99
Indyk, Martin, 36
infrastructure: in Arab countries,
    59, 62, 150; in Occupied
    Territories, 2, 15, 61–62, 133–36
In Search of Palestine, 57–58
intellectuals: Arab, 9–10, 16–20,
    182; exchange among, 9–10,
    16–20, 60; failure of, 190; role
    of, 97–99, 154–55, 187
International Christian Embassy,
    152
Internet, 2, 4, 13, 58, 84;
    commodification of, 97
"In the Penal Colony" (Kafka), 183
Intifada (1987), 24, 36–37, 49
Intifada (2000). *See* Al-Aqsa
    Intifada
Iran, 93, 105, 111, 141, 143
Iraq: Afghanistan compared to,
    119; culture of, 171–72; Gulf
    War (1991), 105, 119, 121;
    pronunciation of, 165; sanctions
    against, 91–93, 105, 172; U.S.
    ignorance of, 190–91; U.S.
    imperialism and, 140–44, 167;

U.S. war against, 153, 167–69,
    171–73, 186; violence by, 64
Islam: after September 11,
    109–10; bigotry against,
    121–24; in Egypt, 126–27;
    fundamentalism, 61–62;
    information on, 129;
    intellectuals and, 154; Iraq as
    cultural center of, 171–72;
    language and, 164–65; in
    Pakistan, 127–28; Sharon's
    Al-Aqsa visit and, 40–43;
    terrorism and, 88–91, 115;
    tolerance of Jews in, 148, 179;
    U.S. ignorance of, 104–6,
    115–16; violence ascribed to,
    91, 122, 145–46, 165
"Islam and the West Are
    Inadequate Banners" (Said),
    108
Islamic Jihad, 61–62
Islamic Salvation Front, 62
Israeli Anthropological
    Association, 12
Israeli Palestinians: activism by, 6,
    10–11, 48–51; land ownership
    prohibited, 32, 47
Italy, 96, 169–70

J

Japan, 33, 52
Al-Jazeera, 170
Jericho, 14
Jerusalem: annexation of, 33, 39,
    42; East, 32, 42, 133;
    interaction in, 5; occupation of,
    32; in the peace process, 43–45,
    46; settlers in, 133; West, 45
Jewish Defense League, x

220   **Culture and Resistance**

Jews: Al-Aqsa Intifada and, 42–43; Christian anti-Semitism and, 148, 152, 179; Israeli governance and, 6, 49, 51–52; land rights and, 32, 47, 49, 140; music and, 23; suffering of, 53, 73, 147–49, 178–82. *See also* anti-Semitism; Holocaust; religion; Zionism
Jordan: censorship in, 3; Iraq and, 91–92; location of, 48; normalization with Israel, 16, 47; shifting borders and, 42, 50, 63; U.S. and, 2
Jordan, June, 180

K

Kafka, Franz, 183–84
Kahan commission, 41
Kaplan, Robert, 115
Karzai, Hamid, 141
Katznelson, Berl, 9
Khalil Sakakini Cultural Center, 160
Khomeini, Ayatollah, 110
kibbutzim, 32
Kinzer, Stephen, 181
Koran, 124, 164
Korea, 33, 52
Kosovo, 93
Kramer, Martin, 177
Kundera, Milan, 182
Kurds, 92–93
Kuwait, 3, 150, 154

L

land: allocation of, 38–39; colonialist expropriation of, 18, 37, 49, 140, 174; as "empty," 21, 52–53, 174; maps of, 22, 38, 58, 72; prohibitions on ownership

of, 32, 47, 49. *See also* displacement
Landau, Uzi, 140
language: bias and, 21, 94, 170, 173–74; culture and, 161, 164–65, 183; study of, 19
Late Night with David Letterman, 115
Lebanon: lack of censorship in, 3; culture in, 172; emigrants from, 78; Israeli invasion of, 41, 105, 143, 147, 160; location of, 48; media on, 85; Palestinian state and, 63; refugees in, 50, 96–97; Said in, 85
Lelyveld, Joseph, 83
Lerner, Michael, 181
Lewinsky, Monica, 89
Lewis, Anthony, 124
Lewis, Bernard, 43, 56, 146
lobbying: power of, 35–36, 72, 142, 144–46; resistance to, 59–60, 61; right wing and, 152
Lockheed Martin, 150
London Review of Books, 86
London Times, 116

M

Ma, Yo-Yo, 25–26
Madrid talks, 81
Magnes, Judah, 7–9
Makiya, Kanan, 182
malnutrition, 133–35
maps, 22, 38, 58, 72
McCall, Carl, 145
McKinney, Cynthia, 145
McVeigh, Timothy, 90
media: on Al-Aqsa Intifada, 73; alternative, 13, 58, 83–84; bias of, 37–38, 57–58, 59–60, 72,

87–88, 139; commodification of, 97; demonization by, 110; "experts" in, 124–26; ignorance of, 3–4; imperialism and, 188–89; language bias of, 165–66, 173; racism in, 82–83, 122–23; suicide bombing focus, 134; uniformity of, 170
Mehta, Zubin, 25
Meir, Golda, ix
Melville, Herman, 108–9
memory, 50–51, 181–83. *See also* storytelling
metaphysics: good vs. evil, 108–10, 189; September 11 and, 113, 114–16
Middle East Forum, 177
migration. *See* displacement
Miller, Aaron David, 36
Moby Dick (Melville), 108–9
Morocco, 3, 59
Mossadegh, Mohammad, 105
Motion Picture Academy, 188
movement building: age and, 79; divestment campaigns and, 151, 173, 175; Intifada (1987), 36–37, 49; need for, 59–61, 75, 76, 77–81; Orwell and, 184–86; protests, 54, 168, 170–71, 194n11; Said in, 193. *See also* Al-Aqsa Intifada
mujahideen, 107, 111, 128
Musharraf, Pervez, 128
music, xi, 23–26, 65, 191
Muslim Alliance, 91
Muslim Brotherhood, 62, 126
Muslims. *See* Islam

N

Nablus, 136

Nader, Ralph, 167
al-Nakba, 13, 31–32
National Post, 82
National Public Radio (NPR), 60, 88
Native Americans, 95
Nazareth, 10, 12
Nazis, 73, 86, 138, 147. *See also* Holocaust
Neruda, Pablo, 163
Netanyahu, Benjamin, 7, 45–46, 55
New Mexican, 73
New Republic, 61, 82, 84, 123
NewsHour, 88
New York Times: on Pakistan, 128; on Palestinians, 15, 58, 73, 84, 173, 176; on Said, 4; Zionist ad in, 74
Nguyen Cao Ky, 93
Nguyen Van Thieu, 93
1984 (Orwell), 185
normalization, 16–19, 21
Northrup Grumman, 150

O

oil trade, 91–92, 93, 142–43
Oklahoma City, Oklahoma, 90–91
Omar, Mullah, 141
one-state solution, 5–7, 63–64, 148–49
Orientalism (Said), x–xi, 82, 122
Orlando Sentinel, 88
Orwell, George, 184–86
Oslo talks: criticism of, x, 3–4; failure of, 6, 139; Labor Party and, 46; land lost during, 81, 96
Out of Place (Said), 65, 192

222   **Culture and Resistance**

P

Pacheco, Allegra, 58
pacifism, 154
Pakistan, 93, 127–28, 129
Palestine Liberation Organization
(PLO): creation of, 51; Darwish
and, 162; Lebanon invasion and,
143; media demonization of,
110; in the peace process, 33, 81,
136; unity and, 50
Palestinian Authority (PA), 14, 18,
59, 75
Palestinian Central Bureau of
Statistics, 160
Palestinian National Council
(PNC), x, 163
Parris, Matthew, 116, 119
Paulin, Tom, 174–76
peace process: failure of, 39, 43–48;
Hebron and, 54; history of, 3–4,
33; infrastructure decline and,
59; Madrid, 81; media focus on,
10; Oslo, x, 3–4, 6, 81, 96, 139;
rebellion against, 37; settlements
and, 43–44, 46, 55, 63; U.S. role
in, 33, 35–36, 39, 53; Wye
agreement, 4
Pen and the Sword, The (Said), xi, 146
Peres, Shimon, 45–46, 55, 94
Peretz, Martin, 82, 84
Perle, Richard, 141–42, 167
Picasso, Pablo, 186
Pipes, Daniel, 177
Plutarch, 191
poetry, xi, 161–64, 166–67, 175–76
Poland, 53
postmodernism, 190
Powell, Colin, 76, 88, 92, 118, 165,
186

protests: Intifada (1987), 36–37,
49; against Iraq war, 168,
170–71, 194n11; by settlers and
Orthodox Israelis, 54. *See also*
Al-Aqsa Intifada

Q

Qabbani, Nizar, 161
Qaddafi, Muammar, 110
al-Qaeda, 140, 141
Qatar, 150
Qibia, 41

R

Rabbo, Yasir Abed, 2
Rabin, Yitzhak, 45–46, 55
racism: against Arabs, 49, 53, 74,
82–83, 122–24, 165–66; in
media, 82–83, 122–23; in U.S.,
91. *See also* anti-Semitism; South
Africa
Ramallah, 134, 160
Rather, Dan, 115
Reagan, Ronald, 107
Reel Bad Arabs (Shaheen), 122
Reflections on Exile (Said), 65, 184
refugees: information on, 31,
65n2, 96; Jewish, 147; massacre
of, 41; right of return, 32,
43–45, 95–96. *See also*
displacement; al-Nakba
religion: Al-Aqsa Intifada and,
42–43; comparisons among,
148; divine right to land, 140;
fundamentalism, 106–8,
151–53, 171; infrastructure and,
61–62; in politics, 6, 11–12, 49,
51–52. *See also* Christianity;
Islam; Jews

Index

223

Report on Israel Settlement in the Occupied Territories, 39
repression, 49, 133–36, 183–84
Rhee, Syngman, 93
Rich, Frank, 125
right of return, 32, 43–45, 95–96
roads, 5, 37, 39, 133
Road to Wigan Pier, The (Orwell), 184
Romania, 137
Rose, Charlie, 43. *See also Charlie Rose Show*
Ross, Dennis, 36, 145–46
Roy, Arundhati, 90
Rumsfeld, Donald, 118, 140, 142, 153

S

Sabra and Shatila massacre, 41
Sadat, Anwar, 126
Safire, William, 84
Said, Edward: Barenboim and, 23–26, 65; censorship of, 2–4, 57–58, 84–87; health of, xi, 27, 64, 192; lectures by, 10–12, 85–87; self-consciousness of, 192; visits to Middle East by, 5, 13–18, 85
Sakakini, Khalil, 160
sanctions against Iraq, 91–93, 105, 172
Saudi Arabia, 3, 107, 142–43, 150, 179
School of Oriental and African Studies, 80
Seattle Post-Intelligencer, 88
self-defense, 34, 136–39
September 11: analysis of, 116–18; context of, 103–8, 111; effects of, 168; just response to, 120–21; other terrorism compared to,

112–13, 114–15; retribution for, 108–10
settlements: displacement by, 32, 37, 55; early, 147; information on, 39–40, 66n4; peace process and, 43–44, 46, 55, 63; population of, 33, 133; protesters from, 54; rate of, 75, 136; separation from Palestinians, 55, 73
Shaheen, Jack, 121–22
Sharon, Ariel: Al-Aqsa mosque visit, 40–43; on assassinations, 138, 156n11; Barak compared to, 75; election of, 71; Lebanon invaded by, 143, 160; metaphysics and, 141; negative attitude of, 137, 139; repression by, 135; U.S. war on terrorism and, 140
Shas Party, 74
Shatila. *See* Sabra and Shatila massacre
Shavit, Avi, 56–57
Shehada, Salah, 156n11
Sheik, The, 123
Silverstein, Hilda, 181
Sinatra, Frank, 10
"Slow Death" (Said), 135
South Africa: compared to Palestine, 7, 40, 60, 73, 75, 173; divestment movement and, 151, 173, 175; Truth and Reconciliation Commission, 52
South Korea, 93
Soviet Union. *See* U.S.S.R.
State Department, 88
storytelling, 20–22, 72, 186–87
"street," 170
Sudan, 89

224 **Culture and Resistance**

suffering, 20–23, 94–95, 180–81
suicide bombing, 112, 134, 138
Suleiman, Elia, 187–88
Summers, Lawrence, 174–76
Sweden, 96–97
Syria, 48, 64, 78, 93, 96

T

Taliban, 107, 111, 128, 141
teaching, 97–98
Telhani, Shibley, 144
terrorism: analysis of, 111–14,
    118–19; ascribed to Palestinians,
    x, 83; domestic, 90–91; Islam
    and, 145–46; Israeli acts
    compared to, 46; state, 111–14;
    suicide bombing, 112, 134, 138;
    U.S. imperialism and, 88–91,
    140–44, 189; Zionist use of,
    34–35, 147. *See also* September
    11
Thailand, 137
Tiananmen Square, 37
Tikkun, 181
torture, 47
"Tourism Among the Dogs" (Said),
    184
Tukan, Fadalla, 163
Tunisia, 3
Turkey, 92–93, 181

U

U.S.S.R., 107, 111, 141, 190
Umm el-Fahm, 49
"Under Siege" (Darwish), 162
United Arab Emirates, 150
United Kingdom: as colonial
    power, 9, 35, 40, 89, 147, 148;
    democracy lacking in, 169, 190;

as distraction, 77; immigration
    laws in, 96; Iraq sanctions by,
    91; contact with Islamic world,
    104; Orwell and, 185; protest
    in, 170; terrorism by, 113; U.S.
    and, 117
United Nations: art at, 186; Israel
    and, 72, 149; importance of,
    81–82; reports by, 88, 173;
    resolutions by, 42, 43, 81–82,
    149; on right of return, 95–96;
    terrorism and, 111, 121; U.S.
    and, 36, 121, 169
United States: anti-Americanism,
    92, 104–8, 144, 153, 168–69,
    177; Arab focus on, 18–19, 76,
    77; Arabs in, 59–60, 78, 82–83;
    arms supplied by, 60–61, 75,
    105, 111, 139, 150–51;
    democracy and, 105–6, 144,
    168, 189; foreign aid, 35, 60,
    74–75, 105, 135–36; Gulf War
    (1991), 105, 119, 121; ignorance
    of, 56, 104–5, 115–16, 135,
    190–91; immigration laws in,
    96–97; imperialism of, 2, 59,
    88–91, 104–7, 140–44, 167–69,
    188–91; Iraq war, 153, 167–69,
    171–73, 186; Israel supported
    by, 48, 50, 139, 149; Jewish
    refugees refused by, 147; Jews
    in, 22, 56, 57, 80; lobbying in,
    35–36, 59–61, 72, 142, 144–46,
    152; media in, 57, 139, 170,
    188–89; mistakes by, 93–94;
    Pakistan and, 127–28; in the
    peace process, 33, 35–36, 39,
    53; sanctions against Iraq,
    91–93, 105, 172; terrorism and,
    88–91, 110–11, 117–21,

140–44, 189; terrorism by, 113; Turkey supported by, 93; UN and, 36, 121, 169
Universal Declaration of Human Rights, 95–96

V

Valentino, Rudolph, 123
Vienna, Austria, 85–87
Vietnam, 93
violence: ascribed to Muslims, 91, 122, 145–46, 165; ascribed to Palestinians, 72, 83, 85, 87–88; assassination, 25, 76, 126, 138, 156n11; casualty rates, 35, 72–73, 134, 137–38; of colonialism, 71–72; against Muslims after September 11, 109–10; against Palestinians in Occupied Territories, 35, 41, 46–47, 54–55, 72–73, 134, 137–38. *See also* arms; terrorism

W

Wagner, Richard, 23
Wall Street Journal, 82
Walzer, Michael, 145, 181
war crimes, 120–21
Washington Post, 58
Weimar, Germany, 25–26
Weizmann, Chaim, 9, 53
Western Washington University, 80
West Jerusalem, 45
Wiesel, Elie, 43
Will, George, 188
Wolcott, Derek, 162
Wolfowitz, Paul, 118, 142, 167
women, 153

World Trade Center. *See* September 11
Wye agreement, 4

Y

Yeats, W.B., 163
Yosef, Ovadia, 74
Yugoslavia, 121

Z

Zionism: American, 56, 57, 80; denial of Palestinians in, 21, 53, 174; goal of, 152; Palestinian study of, 7–9; shortcomings of, for Israelis, 81; terrorism and, 34–35, 147
Z Magazine, 88
Zuckerman, Mort, 82, 125

Photo by Rebecca A. Kandel

About the Authors

Edward W. Said (1935–2003) was born in Jerusalem, Palestine, in 1935 and attended schools there and in Cairo. He received his B.A. from Princeton and his M.A. and Ph.D. from Harvard. He was University Professor at Columbia. Among his many books are *Orientalism, The Question of Palestine, Covering Islam, Culture and Imperialism, Representations of the Intellectual, The Politics of Dispossession, Peace and Its Discontents, Reflections on Exile and Other Essays, The End of the Peace Process, Parallels and Paradoxes: Explorations in Music and Society* (with Daniel Barenboim), and *Freud and the Non-European*. His memoir, *Out of Place*, won the *New Yorker* Book Award for non-fiction in 2000. In 2001, Said received the Lannan Foundation's Literary Award for Lifetime Achievement.

David Barsamian is the founder and director of Alternative Radio in Boulder, Colorado. He has published books with Noam Chomsky, Eqbal Ahmad, Howard Zinn, Tariq Ali, Richard Wolff, and Arundhati Roy, and lectures widely on national and international affairs. Barsamian is the winner of the Media Education Award, the ACLU's Upton Sinclair Award for independent journalism, and the Cultural Freedom Fellowship from Lannan Foundation. The Institute for Alternative Journalism named him one of its Top Ten Media Heroes. His other Haymarket Books titles include *The Pen and the Sword*, with Edward W. Said; *Propaganda and the Public Mind*, with Noam Chomsky; and *Confronting Empire*, with Eqbal Ahmad.

Alternative Radio's Audio Archives

Alternative Radio (AR) is an award-winning, weekly radio program produced in Boulder, Colorado. It is offered free to all public radio stations in the United States and around the world. AR provides information, analyses, and views that are frequently ignored or distorted in corporate-controlled media. Established in 1986, AR is dedicated to the founding principles of public broadcasting, which urge that programming serve as "a forum for controversy and debate," be diverse, and "provide a voice for groups that may otherwise be unheard." The project is entirely independent, sustained solely by individuals who purchase programs.

Ralph Nader calls AR "a ray of light in the media darkness featuring voices of proposals to strengthen our democracy."

AR maintains a large collection of speeches and interviews featuring Edward W. Said, Vandana Shiva, Tariq Ali, Howard Zinn, Arundhati Roy, Michael Parenti, Chris Hedges, and many others. We also house the largest collection of Noam Chomsky offerings in the world. To order, or to view our complete catalog, visit our website, www.alternativeradio.org.

About Haymarket Books

Haymarket Books is a radical, independent, nonprofit book publisher based in Chicago.

Our mission is to publish books that contribute to struggles for social and economic justice. We strive to make our books a vibrant and organic part of social movements and the education and development of a critical, engaged, international left.

We take inspiration and courage from our namesakes, the Haymarket martyrs, who gave their lives fighting for a better world. Their 1886 struggle for the eight-hour day—which gave us May Day, the international workers' holiday—reminds workers around the world that ordinary people can organize and struggle for their own liberation. These struggles continue today across the globe—struggles against oppression, exploitation, poverty, and war.

Since our founding in 2001, Haymarket Books has published more than five hundred titles. Radically independent, we seek to drive a wedge into the risk-averse world of corporate book publishing. Our authors include Noam Chomsky, Arundhati Roy, Rebecca Solnit, Angela Y. Davis, Howard Zinn, Amy Goodman, Wallace Shawn, Mike Davis, Winona LaDuke, Ilan Pappé, Richard Wolff, Dave Zirin, Keeanga-Yamahtta Taylor, Nick Turse, Dahr Jamail, David Barsamian, Elizabeth Laird, Amira Hass, Mark Steel, Avi Lewis, Naomi Klein, and Neil Davidson. We are also the trade publishers of the acclaimed Historical Materialism Book Series and of Dispatch Books.

CPSIA information can be obtained
at www.ICGtesting.com
Printed in the USA
LVHW091501170319
610953LV00007B/83/P